Regional Economic Analysis for Practitioners

Praeger Publishers   New York   Washington   London

PRAEGER PUBLISHERS
111 Fourth Avenue, New York, N.Y. 10003, U.S.A.
5, Cromwell Place, London S.W.7, England

Published in the United States of America in 1972
by Praeger Publishers, Inc.

© 1972 by Praeger Publishers, Inc.

Library of Congress Catalog Card Number: 76-180841

Printed in the United States of America

TO LEAH,

who must never let June go by

Some time ago, the Settlement Study Centre in Rehovot, Israel, asked me to prepare a series of lectures for its International Course in Comprehensive Regional Development Planning. Students in the course were college graduates, but, as a rule, they were not accomplished economists, mathematicians, statisticians, planners, or regional scientists. Most were in early stages of careers as regional development field workers, staff members of regional development authorities, officials of central government agencies concerned with regional development, or the like, and were destined to be very much involved in the practical business of regional development. They therefore had a deep need for an operational familiarity with at least the more common descriptive methods of regional economic analysis in current use.

The students were already familiar with the better-known literature on the subject, but they had found this inadequate for several reasons. First, these works characteristically are addressed not to the level of the field worker, local staff analyst, or government official who works with the local development team, but, rather, to that of the researcher who works at a university or other institution with an interest often more academic than pressing.

Then, too, most of the present literature on the subject of regional economic analysis concerns developed regions or lagging regions within the developed Western world. This has vast implications for the context of the analysis as well as the environment in which it is performed. Further, that part of the existing literature which does concern itself with underdeveloped regions in the context of an underdeveloped country generally is written for the U.S. or European researcher who contemplates the analysis from the developed-research environment with which he is familiar. This environment includes such amenities as computers and computer programers, inexpensive but relatively skilled graduate-assistant labor, foundation research assistance, and access to a wide variety of talents at the Ph.D. level.

Finally, a good portion of the literature is written with a view of the nation as a system of regions. While the importance of this view is unquestioned, it unfortunately usually precludes concern with the detailed analysis needs of a particular region.

The challenge, then, was to put together a package which would enable the students, upon their return home, to apply or to monitor the application of common, analytical methods in the environments of limited skills, manpower, money, and other resources available for regional economic development in their respective countries. Stuffed into the package, it was hoped, would be three elements: First, an element of the conventional; second, an element of the unconventional but well suited to the needs of the students; and third, the tools-- mainly a way of thinking--for adapting the first two elements to the unique requirements of any particular development region. In the end, the package seemed to contain only a limited amount that was entirely new and that had not been said somewhere or sometime before. Clearly, one of its chief values lay in that it was a single package and was packed with a particular kind of address in mind.

This book is based on the lecture series, and, therefore, it is addressed specifically to what I call the regional development "practitioner," of which the students in the International Course are typical. In an attempt to make the book as readable and useful for this audience as I would like it to be, several practices have been adopted that warrant brief explanations, and in some cases, justifications.

In the first place, no attempt is made to define a region. This is a problem with which the practitioner to whom this book is addressed generally is not faced. In most cases the region has been delineated for him by higher authorities; his job is to analyze, and, on the basis of his analysis, to recommend steps for the development of the defined region. In any event, there is no shortage of literature on this particular subject.

Second, the chapters do not flow one from the other. Any chapter can be read as an independent unit. While I would hope that the book is worthy of a complete reading, I believe that the absence of tight interdependence among the chapters makes it more valuable as a working aid.

There are neither notes nor footnotes. It was felt that anything worth saying could be said in the body of the text. Citations are minimized and are accomplished by reference to author entries in chapter sections headed "References."

References have been kept to minimum lengths. However, a long list of literature on subjects covered in this book and on related matters is included as the Bibliography, for readers who wish to probe more deeply, at other levels, and who have the time. Subjects with which most of the entries in the Bibliography concern themselves are obvious by the titles. The Bibliography should be viewed as an extensive introductory reading list in regional economics and methods of regional analysis.

Exercises based on the material presented are provided at the end of each chapter. These are "learning" exercises, designed not to test but to expand the reader's knowledge. They will bear the greatest fruit in group work and self-study, because they have been designed for thinking and not for classroom quiz purposes.

As a means of demonstrating the various analysis methods, simple numerical examples have been fabricated. With their help, the fundamentals of each method can be made quite clear, but, at the expense of realism. It would seem that the only way this problem might be overcome would be to provide an appendix to each chapter that would include a case study in which the method or methods discussed were applied to a real situation. However, detailed descriptions of case-specific applications carry with them the risk of exacerbating rather than ameliorating the problem for most readers. As an alternative, a compromise of sorts, numerical examples in the exercises are a shade more complex than the illustrations in the text. Full-dress case studies will be found among the works listed at the end of each chapter and in the Bibliography.

To those acquainted with the literature of regional economics or regional science, several items will be conspicuous by their absence from this book.

First, regional development theory has not been taken up. A good bit of work has been done in the field of regional economic development theory, and some of it is cited in the Bibliography. It is the purpose of this book neither to advance new theories nor to discuss old ones. However, methods of analysis do not develop in a vacuum, and they generally reflect underlying theories of development. Thus, the reader will be exposed somewhat to this subject, explicitly or implicitly, through discussions on the concepts behind the methods.

Second, planning models have not been presented. The subject of this book is methods of descriptive analysis. These methods employ data that reflect past and present realities; they are designed to help understand what the region is, what changes have taken place, and why. Projection, simulation, and optimization models oriented only toward the future are not covered here. However, many methods for analyzing the past and the present are also good tools for guessing at the future.

Guessing at the future, like analyzing the past and the present, is healthy and useful as an aid to planning regional development. And this use of some of the methods covered will be discussed.

Third, there is no mathematics. All of the methods discussed can be accomplished with arithmetic, in the form in which they are presented. In the case of input-output analysis, the mechanics of the matrix-inverse method and the use of computers are discussed as well. A conscious tradeoff was made between applicability under the conditions mentioned and sophisticated mathematics, with the inclination always toward the former. This does not mean that accuracy or reliability have been sacrificed, and it is hoped, as a result, that the book will be more useful for those to whom it is specifically addressed. Works covering the same methods included in this book but on a more sophisticated mathematical level will be found among those listed in the Bibliography.

Finally, there has been no presentation of analysis from the point of view of the firm or the nation. The assumption is that the material presented in this book will be used by the practitioner at the regional level. While analyses at so-called higher and lower levels are important, and while there is some overlap, they will have to be dealt with as separate subjects elsewhere. Again, the reader who wishes to pursue these points of view will find help among the works listed in the Bibliography.

This book, then, attempts to present simplified means of performing the more common and most widely useful descriptive methods of regional economic analysis. It is aimed at the regional development practitioner who is operating in an environment of limited research resources. I would hope that this effort represents a step in bridging the gap between the high places where such methods are developed and the fields where they find their most important applications.

ACKNOWLEDGMENTS

For their inspiration, assistance, advice, and encouragement, given wittingly or unwittingly, in ways direct and indirect, I am grateful to the following individuals:

Leah Bendavid	Nathaniel Lichfield
Marvin Bendavid	William H. Miernyk
John H. Cumberland	Harvey S. Perloff
Gene Desfor	Frank Piovia
Lene Desfor	William B. Saunders
John R. Friedmann	Arieh Shachar
Morris R. Goldman	Albert Waterston
Morris Hill	Raanan Weitz
Walter Isard	Harold W. Williams
Charles L. Leven	Gideon Witkon

Above all, I am grateful to the staff of the Settlement Study Centre and especially to the students and administration of the International Post-Graduate Course in Comprehensive Regional Development Planning who were present from 1969 to 1972.

CONTENTS

LIST OF FIGURES

Regional Economic Analysis
for Practitioners

1

**INTRODUCTION
TO THINKING
REGIONAL**

FROM NATIONAL TO REGIONAL ECONOMICS

Most students have had at least one or two
basic courses in economics, and these have influenced the way they conceptualize an economy. Generally, these courses have taught students to think
"national," and some reorientation is required for
learning the knack of thinking "regional." This is
not to say that economics at the regional level and
economics at the national (or international) level
are unrelated. Quite the contrary. The former
leans very heavily on the theories and analysis
tools developed for the latter. Thinking regional
requires an appreciation for the points of conver-
gence and for the points of divergence between the
economics of nations and the economics of regions.

As an illustration, consider what is usually
taught in the first hour of an introductory course
in <u>international trade</u>. There, students learn that
trade between countries comes about when, because
of <u>absolute or comparative advantages</u>, both parties
to the trade gain from the exchange. A country may
have production advantages that result from natural-
resource endowments, unique human or institutional

resources, strategic, locational features, or other
scarce, immobile, resource endowments. The greater
the production advantages, the more profitable will
be specialization and trade, and the greater will
be the volume of trade.

These notions can serve as a foundation (upon
which much building must be done) for understanding
interregional trade as well as international trade.
Yet, we know by experience or intuition that in
most cases external trade plays a much greater role
in the economy of a region than in the economy of a
nation. Why is this? What are the barriers to
trade among nations that do not exist, or are not
as serious, at the regional level?

In the first place, distances between national
trading partners are generally greater than among
regions trading within the same country. Clearly,
transportation costs can cancel production advantages in the extreme case, and they often do. De-
fense and political considerations not uncommonly
encourage countries to maintain production capabilities in certain commodities, even though these
might be purchased more cheaply in the international marketplace. National full-employment policies,
strong cultural differences, xenophobia, balance-
of-payments and exchange-rate problems, administrative red tape, and other trade-inhibiting factors
found at the national level are generally absent or
much less intense at the level of trade between
subnational regions. Moreover, and no less important, a nation has the legal tools--tariffs, quotas,
and other institutional barriers--to enforce a re-
striction of trade when it deems this to be in its
best interests. These tools are generally unavailable to regions. With fewer natural and institutional barriers, regions are "free" to specialize
and trade to a much greater degree than nations,
and do.

But not only goods flow more freely across
interregional borders than across international
borders; factors of production that are not fixed

in place by nature--capital, labor, ideas and tech-
niques--also flow more freely. All this gives the
regional economy a quality of <u>openness</u> generally
absent from the national economy.

Thus, we can identify a number of features
that distinguish the economy of the subnational region from that of the nation. Key among these are
a greater degree of specialization and openness, a
closer proximity to trading partners and competi-
tors, and an absence of institutional devices for
"closing" the region at will. These and the fact
that each region is part of a national system of
regions have important implications for the regional economy. We will return to these shortly.

It would be instructive at this point to see
how what we have found thus far would influence the
way we view a <u>national income determination</u> model.
Each of us has buried away in the beginning pages
of our "Fundamentals of Economics" notes a simplified Keynesian commodity-market model of the national economy. This model states that <u>gross national product</u> (GNP) is the sum of domestic consumption spending, private domestic investment
spending, government spending, and net exports (exports less imports). When there is an increase in
any of these components, income increases. Of the
increase in income, part <u>leaks out</u> of the income-
generating stream in accordance with the tax rate,
the marginal propensity to import goods, and the
marginal propensity to save. The remainder enters
the stream of domestic consumption spending and
generates a further increase in income, and the
process is repeated. This goes on, round after
round, until there is nothing left to be spent.

Thus, an initial increase of spending in any
of the GNP components will generate a cumulative
increase in income that is much greater. How much
greater will depend on the magnitude of the <u>multi-
plier</u>, which is calculated as 1 divided by the sum
of the marginal-leakage fractions. For example,
if the value of the multiplier is 1.5, an increase

in spending of Mu. 100 will generate a total increase in income of Mu. 150. (Mu. = monetary
units.) According to the model, then, the larger
the tax rate, the marginal propensity to import,
and the marginal propensity to save, the smaller
will be the multiplier, and, therefore, the total
increase in income generated by the initial increase in spending.

In the commodity-market model, government
spending, domestic investment, and exports are all
determined outside the system. Investment is
linked to the money market through an inverse relationship with the interest rate. We can see the
way the model works by imagining that something in
the money market caused the interest rate to decline. In response, investment spending would increase. The full impact of this increase on income
would be equal to the increase in investment times
the multiplier. If leakages are small, the cumulative impact on income might even be more than
double the initial increase in investment spending.

As before, the model can serve as a foundation
for understanding income determination and multiplier impacts for a region as well as for a nation.
If we were really going to analyze national-income
determination, however, we would want to add quite
a bit more to this foundation. We would consider
the money market as well as the commodity market,
and we would note that government spending is in
fact determined by bodies within the borders of the
economy and is responsive to it. Furthermore, the
"leakages" in the model are not actually "lost" to
the economy. They return, sooner or later, in one
form or another. The only element that is really
determined outside the system, perhaps, is exports;
and the only leakage that is really lost, perhaps,
is imports--and these may be elements of lesser importance in national-income determination.

Now that we have thus made our model more sophisticated and, hopefully, more realistic, we cannot help but be struck by the fact that, as most
national models, it takes the view of the nation as

a more or less closed environment which exists at a
point in space. Income is determined almost entirely by what goes on within the system, and we
need be concerned with only one interest rate, one
level of government spending, one marginal propensity to consume, one multiplier, and so on. What
happens, happens everywhere, as if it all took
place at a single spot.

The features that distinguish a regional from
a national economy (mentioned earlier), imply that
the region is more sensitive to external market
forces with respect to factors of production as
well as goods and services; that fine differences
in spatio-temporal factors play a much greater role
in the regional-production function than is the
case for the nation; that leakages can actually be
"lost" to a region much more readily than to a nation; that feedback impacts, both favorable and un-
favorable, from trade with the "rest of the world"
are much greater for regions; that the region faces
political- and resource-allocation problems of a
nature quite different from the nation because it
competes with other regions within the same national state.

When we consider this, it becomes clear that
income in a region is determined no less, and perhaps more, by what goes on outside the regional
borders than by what goes on within them. Government spending in the region may be determined large-
ly by bodies foreign, at times even hostile, to the
region. A high rate of interest nationally may be
reflected in a flight of capital from the region.
The propensity to consume in the region may be no
less critical than the propensity of the region's
residents to consume. A relatively high national
multiplier may stem from factors that cause the
multiplier of a particular region to be low. An
increase in the regional tax rate relative to other
regions or the country as a whole will mean one
thing; the reverse situation will mean another.

Regional analysis, then, requires a thorough
examination of the region, an examination of the

larger environment of which it is a part, a determination of the natures of the links through which
the two can and do interact, and an evaluation of
the ultimate impacts these interactions have upon
the region.

SOME IMPLICATIONS FOR DEVELOPMENT

The time is ripe for taking the first steps to
relate our ability to think regional to the larger
issue with which we are ultimately concerned, regional development. It will suffice for the present
to consider only two main points.

The first is that there are vast implications
for the development of a region in the fact that
what appears to be good for the nation is not necessarily good for each of its regions, and what is
good for a region is not necessarily good for the
nation. As an illustration, let us suppose that a
plant for the processing of agricultural produce
were established in a rural region which had formerly sent its produce to a distant city, its principal market, for processing. The new plant might
provide employment for regional surplus farm labor
and increase the regional multiplier impact by
eliminating the need to import the processed commodity. It might thereby have an extremely beneficial effect on the level of regional income. However, transfer of the processing to the hinterland
may result in the displacement of higher-paid urban
workers, and, through a negative multiplier effect,
ultimately reduce the GNP. Moreover, the displaced
urban workers who have thus been removed from the
tax base will comprise, together with their families, a greater drain on the public-services budget.

Or, take the example of a national urbaniza-
tion trend that may be looked upon favorably by
government authorities. To their minds, it may reflect a relocation of surplus rural labor that fa-
cilitates a national industrialization program with
a minimum of inflation. The hinterland region,

however, may be losing people from the hamlets and
small towns who perform important services to the
farming population; and the farms may well be losing those who are the ablest, most productive, and
most innovative, or potentially so. In the long
run, the "regional" damage done will have national
implications.

This is not to say that the region must be
viewed as necessarily at odds with the nation. Indeed, proper regional development planning involves
the integration of regional and national development
objectives for the maximum benefit of both. However, because investments made in one region will
mean investments not made in another, and because
it is possible for national and regional interests
to clash, this is not always an easy task.

The second point, hinted at earlier, is that
the institutional tools available for regional development, that is, the administrative and policy-
making bodies and authorities, are quite different
at the regional level from those available at the
national level; and, even if this were not the case,
the same policy alternatives would not be available
at both levels. For example, at the national level,
a reallocation of resources for development can be
brought about by printing money and using it for
development investment. This causes inflation and
a reduction of the demands on resources to satisfy
requirements of consumer-goods production. It is
easy to see that, for better or for worse, such a
policy could not be pursued at the regional level.
And if it were attempted, it would no doubt be relatively ineffective because of diffusion effects
through the region's open borders.

THE DESCRIPTIVE-METHODS APPROACH

We are all familiar with the well-known three-
some of economic factors: land, labor, and capital
--each having a broad interpretation. By now it
should be clear that thinking regional requires
adding the dimension of location.

Descriptive methods of regional analysis provide a means of observing and evaluating the way in
which land, labor, and capital have interacted in
relation to the region's relative location within a
larger system. Through this approach, a region's
unique character can be explained and understood,
and the implications of its past and present for
future development will be revealed.

REFERENCES

1. J. R. Boudeville. "A Survey of Recent
Techniques for Regional Economic Analysis," in
Walter Isard and John H. Cumberland, eds., Regional
Economic Planning (Paris: Organization for Euro-
pean Economic Cooperation, 1961), pp. 377-98.

2. Henry W. Broude, "The Significance of Regional Studies for the Elaboration of National Economic History," Journal of Economic History, XX
(December, 1960), 558-96.

3. John Friedmann, Regional Development
Policy: A Case Study of Venezuela (Cambridge,
Mass.: Massachusetts Institute of Technology Press,
1966).

4. John Friedmann and W. Alonso, eds., Regional Development and Planning (Cambridge, Mass.:
Massachusetts Institute of Technology Press, 1964).

5. Werner Z. Hirsch and Sidney Sonenblum,
Selecting Regional Information for Government Planning and Decision-Making (New York: Praeger Publishers, 1970).

6. Edgar M. Hoover, The Location of Economic
Activity (New York: McGraw-Hill, 1948).

7. Walter Isard, Methods of Regional Analysis:
An Introduction to Regional Science (New York:
Massachusetts Institute of Technology and Wiley,
1960).

8. L. Needleman, ed., <u>Regional Analysis</u> (Harmondsworth, England: Penguin Books, 1968).

9. Hugh Nourse, <u>Regional Economics</u> (New York: McGraw-Hill, 1968).

10. Harvey S. Perloff <u>et al</u>., <u>Regions, Re-sources, and Economic Growth</u> (Baltimore: Johns Hopkins Press for Resources for the Future, 1960).

11. Resources for the Future, <u>Design for a Worldwide Study of Regional Developments</u>, a report to the United Nations on a proposed research-training program (Baltimore: Johns Hopkins Press, 1966).

12. Horst Siebert, <u>Regional Economic Growth</u>: <u>Theory and Policy</u> (Scranton, Pa.: International Textbook Company, 1969).

13. Robert G. Spiegelman, <u>Review of Tech-niques of Regional Analysis with Particular Empha-sis on Applicability of Those Techniques to Region-al Problems</u>, SRI Project No. 532-531-4 (Menlo Park: Stanford Research Institute, 1962).

EXERCISES

1. It has been determined that an increase in the rate of investment is needed as one aspect of a development program. You are a development official. What are the different considerations that come to mind as you contemplate the steps you might take in the case of a nation on the one hand, and of a subnational region on the other? Are the same policy alternatives open in both cases? Why? Give examples.

2. How is it possible for an enterprise to be desirable, on net, from the national perspective, and undesirable, on net, from the viewpoint of the subnational region in which it is located?

3. Labor mobility is generally considered essential for a vigorous economy. Discuss a case in which, while beneficial to the nation's economy, labor mobility can do permanent and extreme damage from a subnational region's point of view.

4. One study claimed to have found that large, diversified, metropolitan areas, such as New York, tend to have multipliers of about 1.8, and that a multiplier of 1.3 has been drived for small, modestly diversified, metropolitan areas. It could be argued that an increase in the multiplier is an important goal of economic development, as it would seem to imply that more of the benefits of spending are passed on to the domestic or local population. Can the comparative level of the multiplier for a subnational region, therefore, be taken as one indicator of regional progress toward economic vigor? What would you expect the multiplier to be in a poor agricultural region? What might happen to the multiplier as agricultural incomes rise? What would the change indicate? What steps could be taken to improve the regional-multiplier impact?

2

THE BASIC
REGIONAL,
STATISTICAL
COMPENDIUM

INTRODUCTION

Data collection is often one of the first and
major tasks of a regional-development authority.
It is a task that can be costly in time, manpower,
and development funds. If the collection is not
performed systematically, it will later be found
that some data obtained are useless and that some
that are needed have not been obtained. And, in
the end, available data may determine the nature of
the analyses performed, instead of the other way
around. It is desirable, then, prior to the collection of detailed data, to work out a preliminary
analysis framework. This framework may be made up
of several analysis methods, such as those found in
the following chapters, each designed to provide
the basis for a deeper understanding of a particular aspect of the regional complex.

Even before a framework of analysis methods
can be contemplated seriously, however, some preparatory work must be done to provide the development
team with a broad familiarity of the region and a
basis for determining the types of analysis tools
needed and feasible. This preparatory work can and

often does take the form of a <u>basic regional, statis-</u>
<u>tical compendium</u>. "Statistical compendium" refers
to a document composed of statistical tables, perhaps accompanied by diagrams, charts, maps, and explanatory text, and covers a wide range of subjects
important to a preliminary understanding of a region's unique nature.

FUNCTIONS OF THE COMPENDIUM

A <u>regional profile</u> in the form of a statistical compendium has the potential to fulfill a great
many functions. It can serve to help present the
region's case to agencies of the central government
and other potential sources of development resources,
and it provides concrete evidence that development
work is in progress. For the local, educated leadership, whose support is essential for the development effort, the compendium provides an introduction to the broad array of regional problems and
potentials.

For the development staff, the completed compendium will not only provide the basis for selecting areas for further intensive study, but it will
also facilitate a preliminary, over-all analysis of
the region and the establishment of initial planning
and implementation priorities.

The task of planning and assembling the compendium often constitutes the first effort that has a
tangible and immediate objective and that requires
the coordinated participation of the entire development staff. As such, the effort helps crystalize
working relationships and areas of specialization
among staff workers. Beyond this, the execution of
the compendium forces a first systematic review of
the entire regional complex by the development team,
brings about first contacts with concerned bodies
in the region, familiarizes the staff with sources
of regional data, and helps in the identification
of types and characteristics of data available and
unavailable for future reference.

Of course, it is desired that the completed
compendium provide a comprehensive regional charac-
terization, highlight problems and potential solution areas, and thereby constitute the basis for a
preliminary determination of development priorities.
Some of the potential functions of the basic regional, statistical compendium, however, may have
conflicting requirements. If it is to be used to
help generate local enthusiasm for the development
effort, for example, it must be readily intelligible
and meaningful to the local, educated leadership.
This may be in conflict with the requirements im-
plied if it is to be of good analytical value to
the development staff. The tradeoff that will be
required between the variety of functions which the
completed compendium can fulfill, on the one hand,
and its adequacy for planning-oriented analysis, on
the other, should be made consciously and should be
reflected in the compendium design.

COMPONENTS OF COMPENDIUM TABLES

Usually, the maps, charts, diagrams, and text
of a regional compendium are based on the statistical tables that make up the heart of the document.
When we consider how the set of tables might be designed, we find that there are four basic structural
components concerning which decisions must be made.
These components which receive expression on the
face of every table in the compendium set are as
follows (see Figure 1):

1. Over-all compendium organization--the selection of compendium divisions, or broad subject
categories, and the arrangement of tables within
each of these divisions.

2. Table titles--the specific subjects dealt
with by the tables within each division.

3. Column headings--the specific data selected
to describe the subject with which each table is
concerned.

4.   Table stubs--the row headings that comprise the list of geographic areas for which the
datum indicated in each column heading is provided.

FIGURE 1

Illustration of a Compendium Table
and Its Components

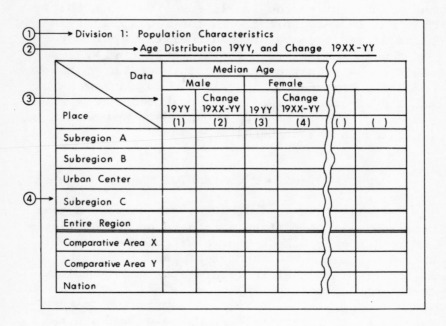

Tables do not have to follow the format of the
illustration in Figure 1. But whatever the format
design, the components remain essentially the same.
And decisions made regarding them will determine
the quality and quantity of information that will
be communicated by the statistical data, that is,
the type of representation of the region which the
completed tables provide.

CONSIDERATIONS IN COMPENDIUM ORGANIZATION
AND SELECTION OF TABLE SUBJECTS

There are a number of possible ways in which
the statistical tables can be organized. One government agency in the United States grouped the
tables in its regional, statistical compendiums according to the following framework:

    Division 1. Profile of the Poor
    Division 2. Geographic Profile
    Division 3. Demographic Profile
    Division 4. Economic Profile
    Division 5. Social Profile

Another agency of the U.S. government developed a
compendium format for multicounty "districts" that
was also organized into five divisions but along
different lines:

    Division 1. Population Characteristics
    Division 2. Economic Structure and Activities
    Division 3. Characteristics of the Unemployed
    Division 4. Physical Resources
    Division 5. Community Facilities

In each of these cases, the broad subject categories
into which the tables are organized reflect the
orientation and specific mission of the agency.

Many studies have used the "regional resources"
approach to over-all compendium organization.   In
this case, the tables might be organized into divisions such as human resources, mineral resources,
timber resources, power resources, institutional
resources, and so on.

The point of all this is that the organization
of a statistical compendium into divisions, or subject categories, is not merely a matter of arbi-
trarily assorting unassorted data. The way in which
the tables are grouped into subject categories
brings about the presentation of data in a manner
that promotes viewing the region in accordance with

a certain analytical orientation. It therefore reflects the intentional or unintentional selection
of a basic approach to regional analysis on the
part of the compendium's authors.

The selection of specific subjects with which
the tables will deal will be dictated in part by
the over-all model organization, in part by the
specific needs of the region under study, and in
part by data availability.

For example, if the regional-resources approach
is selected, this would imply the need, among others,
for a set of tables on power resources, including
hydroelectric, gas, nuclear, and other power resources. However, not all of these necessarily
would be appropriate in a particular region, nor
would data concerning those which were appropriate
necessarily be available.

The table titles will also reflect what the research staff considers to be important within each
broad subject category in the early stages of analysis represented by the statistical compendium.

Chapter 1 makes it clear that to understand
the unique character of a region requires consideration of its relative location within a larger system as well as of the conventional economic factors.
Because a meaningful compendium design must attempt
to bring the relevant regional issues to light, the
selection of major subject categories and the specific tables that each includes should seek to highlight not only what goes on within the region but
also how this is related to the region's locational
characteristics. The locational characteristics
have both a physical dimension and a relative,
spatial dimension.

Thus, a meaningful, regional, tabular profile
might be organized into six divisions, as in Figure
2. The framework presented in Figure 2 also sug-
gests the types of tables that might be included in
each division and provides a brief summary of the

contribution of data in each division toward a comprehensive, regional description.

Figure 2 is suggested only as a broad guide. The central column in the figure should not be misinterpreted as a list of actual table titles nor as an exhaustive checklist of information needed for a "good" statistical compendium. The list is intended merely as an indication of the types of subjects that might be dealt with in each division. It will be noted that the subjects listed are not on a consistent level of detail. For certain regions, a number of the suggested types of tables may not be applicable, and data for many of the tables indicated may not be available. For most regions, the list of table subjects included in each division of the illustration would have to be considerably modified as part of the task of designing a unique compendium framework suitable for the local, regional economy.

It should be noted that grouping the tables into the subject categories suggested in Figure 2 would, for completeness within each division, require that certain tables, or parts of them, appear in more than one division. There is, in fact, some overlap in subject matter among the divisions as they have been laid out in the illustration. Repetition and overlap are not problems. Indeed, they can serve to make the information presented in the model more meaningful by avoiding artificial separation of data that naturally complement each other.

CONSIDERATIONS IN THE DESIGN
OF COLUMN HEADINGS

The design of the column headings of a table reflects the selection of measures and indicators thought most appropriate for describing the subject with which the table deals, from among those for which data are available. Column headings may call for absolute measures, such as regional income; and

FIGURE 2

Organization of a Regional, Statistical Compendium

Division number and title (subject category characteristics).	Division would include but not be limited to tables covering subjects such as these.	Completed tables would provide insights regarding the following.
1. Population and social characteristics	Population size, age distribution, family characteristics, vital statistics, growth components, etc. Education Work experience Income and wealth Personal income and expenditure patterns (sources and uses) Employment and unemployment, labor-force participation, worker-total population ratio, etc. Health, living conditions, etc. Welfare Government Subsets, e.g., farmers, minorities, rural population, urban population, etc.	Status, problems, and potentials of human resources; social organization; local culture, etc.
2. Location	Physical resources Other natural geographic, locational, climatic, etc. features Social capital, infrastructure, and rates and sources of investment in these Governments Inter- and intraregional orientations and spatial relationships Transportation/communication mixes and links	Spatial and physical qualities of the location, both natural and manmade, including general inter- and intra-regional lines of communication and commerce and central-place hierarchy patterns

3. Economic activities	Gross regional product Productivity Sales Farm characteristics Detailed characteristics of major economic activities Investments and capital accumulation Capital/output ratios Industry-mix characteristics	Levels and types of economic activities, industrial linkages, producer or consumer goods orientations, local and export consumption orientations, investment, credit, and other aspects of the region's structure of economic activities
4. Population-location relationships	Population extent, density, and frequency measures, e.g., population per square mile, location and extent of population centers, distribution of settlements by population size, distribution of population by settlements and settlement size, etc. Travel patterns Commutation External travel Migration Land-ownership patterns	The manner in which the characteristics of the population and of the location result in and result from interactions between them
5. Population-activity relationships	Employment by industry Income and wages by industry Unemployment by industry experience Labor/capital ratios Labor productivity by industry	How efficiently human resources are being utilized in economic activity, and the benefit to the population from engaging in the activities and utilizing the technologies prevailing in the region
6. Location-activity relationships	Location of commerce and industry Intra- and interregional flows and linkages Trade areas Labor-market areas Special relationships with other regions	The characteristics, problems, and potentials of economic activity as related to and determined by spatial and physical features of the regional location

they may call as well for <u>processed data</u> computed
from absolute measures, such as percentage increases
in regional income.

Processed data usually involve a comparison of
absolute measures over time or over space, For
<u>intertemporal comparisons</u>, most regional, statisti-
cal compendiums have found percentage or absolute
change over a period or on an annual, average basis
adequate. Here, as with the basic absolute measures,
compendium designers have only to contemplate the
form of expression from among those commonly used
and widely known that would provide the most meaningful, intertemporal comparison in light of the
nature of the subject with which the table deals
and the point to be made.

The percentage change over a period is, of
course, basically nothing more than a <u>ratio compu-
tation</u>. The ratio can be used also to assign a
statistical value to <u>interareal</u> comparisons. Some-
how, this rather simple notion often has been overlooked, with the result that the significance of an
interareal comparison is missed completely.

Figure 3 shows comparative unemployment rates
for a region, for the province in which it is located, and for the nation. On casual observation,
the figures in the two left columns indicate that
while the rates of unemployment in the region and
in its province showed some improvement between the
two years, both compared quite unfavorably with the
national rate of unemployment throughout.

On the right side of Figure 3, national indexes have been computed by dividing the national,
regional, and provincial unemployment rates by that
of the nation for each year and multiplying by 100.
It can be seen readily that unemployment in the region was not simply "higher," or even "much higher,"
than in the nation, but that it was exactly 2.5
times as great. Further, a fact is highlighted by
the national indexes that might otherwise have been
overlooked, namely, that the rate of unemployment

in the province actually worsened somewhat over the period, while that of the region remained virtually constant, <u>relative to the nation</u>. The significance of this finding remains for the regional analyst to contemplate.

FIGURE 3

Illustration of Interareal Indexes

	Unemployment Rates			
			National Indexes	
	19XX	19YY	19XX	19YY
Region	11.3	9.5	251	250
Province	7.8	6.8	173	179
Nation	4.5	3.8	100	100

The meaningfulness of an index may be called into question when the numerator and denominator of the ratio are not entirely independent of each other, or do not at least behave as if they were independent. The appropriate circumstances for using various comparison techniques is a matter for consideration in each specific case. The point to be emphasized is that once an interareal comparison is decided upon, it is usually not enough to show only the comparative figures. In most cases, considerable additional insight can be gained by providing the comparison with a statistical value, of which the interareal index is an example.

CONSIDERATIONS IN THE DESIGN OF TABLE STUBS

The geographic areas listed in the table stub (row headings) include not only the region's towns

and subregions but also the <u>reference areas</u> selected
as <u>norms</u>. These in turn provide a background against
which to consider local data.

National figures are popular as standards of
comparison, and this is reasonable because national
figures reflect the larger environment of which the
region is a part. But for many regions, particularly rural ones, national socioeconomic measures are
often of questionable comparative value. In the
first place, the major component in the calculation
of national figures may be an urbanized population
whose tastes, needs, standards, and way of life in
general are very different from those prevailing in
the nonurbanized areas. Second, a comparison with
the national average, median, or the like, while in
a sense a comparison with a national "composite,"
is not a comparison with anything that exists.
People concerned with economic development at the
local level most frequently view their region and
its progress relative to other, similar regions.
After all, as one local development official put it,
"Not a person in my province has ever migrated to
the national average. They'll move to another province every time."

In many cases, then, other reference areas are
needed as standards of comparison in addition to or
instead of the nation. This is particularly important when the chosen norms will serve as bases for
target setting. Declared development targets must
be realistic and must be based on the values and
aspirations of the region's residents.

There is a wide variety of alternatives to the
national norm as a standard of comparison. Other
possible reference areas include other regions,
medians or averages of all other regions, medians
or averages of selected groups of other regions,
and so on. In the search for a standard of comparison to complement or replace the nation in the stub
of a particular table, the analyst may look for
real or fictitious (composite) areas that are similar to the region under study in terms of population

size or social and cultural characteristics or that
have a functional similarity. As before, the standard of comparison that would be most meaningful
would depend on the subject with which the table
deals and the point to be made.

CONCLUDING REMARKS

Some factors critical to an understanding of a
region and its past and potential (future) development may not lend themselves to quantification or
to presentation in a tabular format, even of the
simple type discussed in this chapter. This may be
especially true in regions in early stages of development where, for example, factors such as social
mobility and stratification can be decisive in development efforts but may resist meaningful expression in statistical form. And it may be true with
regard to certain aspects of the quality of the
human environment for regions in any stage of development. Therefore, in some cases, it may be advisable to arrange for a special supplement to the
statistical compendium to deal with nonquantifiable
social, cultural, institutional, environmental, or
other aspects of the regional fabric.

REFERENCES

Reference material in English that bears directly on the subject of this chapter in a manner relevant to the working environments of the main body of
readers is scanty, at best. Readers are referred to
Chapter 1 and its References for the regional orientation necessary for preliminary planning of a regional, statistical compendium. In addition, the
following references are recommended.

1. W. Kawalec, "Regional Statistics for Planning Requirements," Paper presented at the Conference of European Statisticians, Prague, 1967.

2. U.N. Research Institute for Social Development, <u>Case Studies in Information Systems for Regional Development</u>, Vol. I, Tormod Hermansen, <u>Sweden</u>; Vol. II, Sergio Boisier, <u>Chile</u>; and <u>India</u> and <u>Poland</u>, forthcoming (Geneva: U.N. Research Institute for Social Development, 1970).

3. U.S. Department of Health, Education, and Welfare, <u>Toward a Social Report</u> (Washington, D.C.: U.S. Government Printing Office, 1969).

EXERCISES

1. Suggest an alternate way to that provided in Figure 2 for organizing the tables of the regional, statistical compendium. Provide samples of the tables you would include in each major subject category of your alternate design.

2. Consider Figure 3 and the discussion surrounding it. Work up a numerical example based on data from your own region and country that demonstrates the same point (your example need not deal with unemployment).

3. Suppose your country is composed of five regions. One is urban, contains 30 percent of the total population, and has an annual, average, family money income about four times that prevailing in the rural regions. The other four regions are agricultural and are of about equal size in population. No precise determination of the size of in-kind incomes to rural families has been made, but they are known to be significant. If you are working with a rural region, what might be an appropriate norm for comparison?

The nation (national averages)?
The rural subspace (rural averages)?
The median region (median regional values)?
The median rural region (median rural regional values)?
Some other, or a combination?

Explain your choice, and explain why certain norms might be appropriate for some subjects that are being investigated but not for others. Give examples.

4. Division 2 of Figure 2 concerns location characteristics. One of the subjects in this division is "Inter- and intraregional orientations and spatial relationships." One useful table dealing with this subject might be entitled "Regional Market Centers and Potential Market Centers Outside the Region, by Highway Distances." For each major

market center in the region (in many cases there
will be only one), this table would show the real
or potential market area by highway distances, and
distances along major routes to other market centers, both within and outside the region. What re-
strictions would you place on the scope of such a
table in order to make it manageable yet meaningful?
Provide a suggested design for the table that shows
how the column headings and stub would appear.

3

**INCOME MEASURES
AND REGIONAL,
SOCIAL ACCOUNTING**

INTRODUCTION

This chapter deals with regional income measures and regional social accounting. The latter term actually covers a wide range of analysis tools, some of which are covered in other chapters of this book. In this chapter, the terms social accounts and regional accounts refer to income and product accounts, or variations of them. Because these variations are limited only by the analyst's imagination, they sometimes lose much of their resemblance to conventional income and product accounts.

Because we must start somewhere, and because to start at the beginning would require more space than is available, the discussion in this chapter assumes a basic familiarity with national income accounting procedures. The reader for whom this term is foreign, and to whom GNP and NNP sound like radio call letters, is advised to review the chapters on national income in any good economics textbook.

Familiarity with accounting procedures at the national level is important because these serve as

the point of departure for designing regional accounts. And regional income measures, although
they may appear to be conceptually simpler, derive
explicitly or implicitly from regional accounts.

Regional income measures provide indications
of personal and community welfare and economic
growth. Regional social accounts can be designed
to provide the same thing and much more. They can
be a powerful tool for description and analysis of
a region's economic structure and are capable of explicitly reflecting an underlying social, ethnic,
geographic, or other substructure, in the bargain.

A change in real income is usually taken to imply a change in welfare in the same direction. But
a number of important theoretical issues arise when
using measures of income as indicators of welfare.
Does an increase in income always mean an increase
in welfare for the individual and for the community?
And does the absence of an increase in income always
imply that personal and community welfare has not
increased and that progress in economic development
has not taken place? While the change in regional,
personal income is by definition the sum of the
changes in the incomes of persons in the region,
can the same be said with regard to the changes in
regional and personal welfare? What are the relative roles of public (collective) goods and services,
on the one hand, and individual command over private
(consumption) goods and services, on the other, in
the determination of personal and community welfare?
To what extent do the social costs (environmental
contamination, cultural disruption, etc.) involved
in producing increased income lessen the increased
welfare that the increase in income supposedly reflects? How can meaningful recognition be made of
nonmonetary (in-kind) income? What is the relationship between income, a flow concept, and wealth, a
stock concept, as regards personal and community
welfare and regional development?

There is a rich literature that addresses
these and other questions regarding the relationships

among income, welfare, and regional development.
The reader can obtain help in this area from the
References at the end of this chapter and from the
Bibliography at the end of the book. Here, it will
be sufficient to point out that the very fact that
such fundamental questions continue to trouble economists and other social scientists is strong indication that measures of income, and even detailed social accounts, alone are inadequate (albeit very important) indicators of personal and community welfare and of progress in economic development.

Happily, there is also a rich literature on
the techniques and concepts of regional income and
social accounting. Again, the reader is urged to
make use of the References and Bibliography to en-
rich his background on the subject. In particular,
Chapter 4 of Isard (1960), is "must" reading. The
task of the present chapter is to highlight some
fundamentals and provide examples of various ap-
proaches to regional, social accounting.

BASIC INCOME MEASURES

The basic income measures employed by analysts
at the regional level are, for the most part, coun-
terparts of those commonly employed at the national
level. They do not always have the same analytical
usefulness, however, and because of data-collection
difficulties, computation of regional income measures is generally more problematic.

Figure 4 provides the conceptual framework
upon which the computation of regional income measures is based, explicitly or implicitly. Gross
regional product (GRP), is the total value, at market prices, of final goods and services produced in
the region during the accounting period, usually one
year. The word "final" means that the goods and
services are not purchased for further processing
or resale within the region.

FIGURE 4

Regional Income Computations, Conceptual Scheme

	Gross regional product (at market prices)
less:	Capital consumption allowances of enterprises in the region
equals:	Net regional product
less:	Business (including government enterprises) payments other than those to or on behalf of local factors of production
plus:	Subsidies to enterprises in the region
equals:	Regional income (paid to local factors of production)
less:	Regional income not accruing to persons
plus:	Other income accruing to persons residing in the region
equals:	Regional personal income
less:	Personal taxes paid by residents of the region
equals:	Regional disposable income
less:	Personal consumption expenditures of residents of the region
equals:	Personal savings of residents of the region

GRP can be computed by adding up personal consumption expenditures in the region, private investment in the region, local and central government expenditures in the region, and all sales outside the
region (exports), and then subtracting the value of
goods and services purchased outside the region and
resold in the region or used as inputs to the region's production (imports). One could also use
total expenditures, not only those in the region,
of local persons, firms, and governments, plus all
expenditures by foreigners in the region; but then
imports would include all purchases outside the region, not simply those used for resale or as inputs.
Alternatively, the value, at market prices, of final
goods and services produced in the region by each
industry category (less the value of imported inputs),
or the value added by each industry category, could
be summed to obtain the gross product of the region
for the accounting year.

Figure 4 begins with GRP and deducts the various charges against it (the cost incurred in the
production of goods and services). One of the costs
of production is the using up of capital that must
be replaced. When capital-consumption allowances
are netted out of gross regional product, the resulting figure is net regional product (NRP).

However, the value of goods and services at
market prices is not identical with income to factors of production, because some of the costs of
production (such as indirect business taxes) do not
represent payments to factors. When all business
payments other than those to or on behalf of factors of production are deducted and subsidies to
enterprises in the region are added in, the resulting figure is regional income, which reflects the
actual earnings accruing to factors of production
in the region in consequence of the production of
gross regional product.

Regional personal income includes that part of
regional income that people take home in the form
of personal earnings, from all sources, before

taxes. Thus, from regional income must be deducted
social insurance contributions, corporate income
taxes, retained corporate profits, and the like.
But it also includes income from other sources, such
as dividends, which must then be added in.

When personal taxes are deducted from regional
personal income, the resulting figure is regional
disposable income. Disposable income can be dis-
posed of in only two ways, spending or saving. Disposable income must not be confused with discretion-
ary income. The latter term is generally taken to
refer to disposable income minus payments due on
commitments made previously. However, in the context of an underdeveloped region, commitments made
previously might meaningfully include minimum sub-
sistence expenditures, such as those for basic food
and shelter.

Regional percapita income is usually based on
regional personal income or regional disposable income and is simply income divided by population.

Any of these income measures can be computed
by building up or by breaking down. Thus, the regional analyst can begin by estimating gross regional product by a building-up procedure involving
estimation and then summation of the various expenditure or production components. He then proceeds to
a breaking-down process in order to arrive at various income measures. Or he may do it the other way
around and begin with disposable income or personal
income estimates.

Two important income measures that cannot be
arrived at through the scheme presented in Figure 4
are median family (or household) income and median
family (or household) percapita income. The former
is simply the midpoint in the array of all the family (or household) incomes in the region, such that
50 percent of the families have an income which is
greater, and 50 percent have an income which is
lesser. The latter measure is computed by dividing
the former by the region's average family (or

household) size. This yields the income available
to each member of the family or household with the
median income.

Average family income has not been mentioned
because its analytical value is identical with that
of percapita income.

CONSIDERATIONS CONCERNING
BASIC INCOME MEASURES

Each of the income measures mentioned has its
particular advantages and disadvantages as an indicator of individual and community welfare and as an
indicator of progress in economic development both
in absolute terms and in relative terms through
interareal and intertemporal comparisons. We now
turn to a brief discussion of these.

Gross regional product, as the most comprehensive measure, has obvious advantages and perhaps
less obvious disadvantages. There is a widespread
tendency to attribute more significance to GRP than
it warrants. It must be remembered that this measure only provides an estimate of the money value
of economic activity originating in the region, but
it says nothing about the quality of that activity.
Furthermore, it may have widely varying values, de-
pending on how that activity is measured. Economists
like to tell the story about the man who married his
housekeeper and thereby reduced the GNP because he
no longer purchased her services, although the services she provided remained the same (very generally
speaking, of course). There is more warning than
wit in the story, the point of which is that GRP
measures what GRP measures, and nothing more. That
this be defined as the money value of final goods
and services produced in the region does not make
it so, does not ensure that it is comparable with
GRP computed for other regions, and is not sufficient cause to conclude that an increase in GRP indicates embarkation on the road of continued economic growth.

The same comments apply to <u>net regional product</u>.
This measure is particularly useful in conjunction
with gross regional product because a comparison of
the two highlights the portion of the region's production that originates with capital consumption.
In other words, the difference between gross regional product and net regional product represents
a portion of revenues that will have to be allocated
to capital replacement in order to maintain a constant level of output, if nothing else changes.

Both gross regional product and net regional
product may be computed on a percapita basis. Such
a computation provides an additional dimension to
the analytical value of these measures for interareal
and intertemporal comparisons. However, if the com-
parability of GRP or NRP figures for different areas
is in question to begin with, conversion to a percapita basis does not improve the situation.

<u>Regional income</u> is an important measure because
it represents the earnings of local factors of production resulting from the parts they played in producing gross regional product. Accordingly, the
change in regional income is a more accurate reflection than the change in GRP or NRP of the impact on
the earnings and welfare of the region's residents--
both individuals and organizations--of a change in
the region's production. Again, the measure takes
on added significance when compared with gross regional product and highlights the difference in the
value of regional production in terms of revenues
obtained in the marketplace, on the one hand, and
the portion of those revenues accruing as income to
local factors of production, on the other.

<u>Regional personal income</u> is of the utmost im-
portance because it provides a more direct indication of that with which the regional developer is
ultimately concerned, the welfare of people. However, the welfare of people and economic development may not be one and the same thing, in the
short run. A change in regional personal income is
the net result of the participation of the human

factor of production in a changing regional product
and changes in income from sources unrelated to the
region's production. Thus, an inmigration of unem-
ployed into a region may result in an increase in
regional personal income stemming from increased
welfare payments. Without a knowledge of what is
behind the increase, the measure can be quite mis-
leading if used as an indicator of regional development, and, therefore, of prospects for long-run
increases in personal welfare.

    Regional disposable income provides an indica-
tion of individual command over goods and services
and is particularly useful as an interareal or intertemporal comparative indicator. A comparison of
the changes in regional personal income and regional
disposable income highlights the portions of the
change in personal income available for public goods,
on the one hand, and private goods, on the other.
This can be of substantial importance in regional
development policy decisionmaking.

    A change in income in a region is brought about
by changes in the incomes earned by people and by
changes in the number of people earning incomes.
The value of percapita income measures is that they
register changes only when--and to the extent that--
there is a disparity between the rate of growth in
the region's income and the rate of growth in the
region's population. It is, of course, entirely
possible, over a given period, that income in a region may show impressive growth, but the population
of the region grows by an even greater proportion.
In such a case, percapita income would help in understanding the true significance of the relative
changes by registering a decline for the period.
While it provides some indication of changes in individual welfare, percapita income does not provide
the analyst with any insight into the distribution
of income. Thus, if income and population in a region were to remain unchanged over a period but
there were to be a shift from a highly skewed income distribution to a relatively even one, percapita income would remain constant; and, on the

basis of this measure alone, the analyst would be
unaware of a development of major importance for
the future of the region.

Median family (or household) income provides
an indication of income distribution and how this
distribution changes over time. It becomes an exceptionally useful income measure when supplemented
by the maximum and minimum figures for the range of
incomes in the region. However, for the insight
into income distribution that this measure provides,
a price appears to have been paid, because total income in the region cannot be computed from median
income data. In practice, however, the type of survey upon which median family or household income
estimates would be based could be designed to supply information upon which total income (and therefore percapita income) estimates could be based as
well, with virtually no extra effort.

In many countries, substantial differences in
average family size have been found to exist among
regions. Furthermore, many regions have shown
dramatic changes in average family size over relatively brief periods. These observations bring
into question the meaningfulness of median family
(or household) income as a measure, particularly
for interareal or intertemporal comparisons. Median
family (or household) percapita income overcomes
these possible objections in much the same way that
percapita computations facilitate more meaningful
comparisons of regional disposable income and regional personal income. However, in working with
median family (or household) percapita income,
sight is lost of the median income of the basic
economic unit (the family or household), a datum
that retains substantial analytical value despite
its shortcomings. Again, in practice, this problem
may be more apparent than real, for both measures
can be computed easily enough from the same data.
Median family (or household) income and median family (or household) percapita income, and changes in
them, are most useful when considered together, as
complements.

The alert reader has by now concluded for him-
self that because each of the basic income measures
focuses on a particular aspect of the total regional
income picture, the selection of one or more measures must be a function of the use to which the information is to be put. And because each measure
has its distinct advantages and disadvantages, the
measures can provide maximum analytical value only
when each is considered in light of the others.

Given the full array of regional income measures, the regional analyst would still be less than
fully satisfied. He would want to delve deeper, to
consider the disaggregated components of the income
measures, and through an analysis of the structure
of the economy, draw conclusions concerning development potentials. To this end, he would seek the
full set of regional social accounts behind the income measures.

DEVISING A SET OF REGIONAL ACCOUNTS

The regional accounts can be any set of bal-
anced accounts that cover the economic activity of
the region, or a component of that activity, in
greater or lesser detail. They may be organized
along any desired lines in accordance with analytical needs and data availability.

Generally, in devising a set of regional accounts, national accounting procedures serve as a
starting point. The main justification for this is
that they are there, and they constitute a familiar
and convenient double-entry accounting system. It
would be useful for analytical purposes to have a
set of regional accounts comparable to the national
accounts, but to accomplish this usually requires
revision of the national accounts in the image of
those devised for the region. For regional accounts generally cannot be meaningfully patterned
precisely after national accounts.

This is so because of several factors. In the
first place, the regional economy is basically an

open one, while the national economy is relatively
closed. This means that at the regional level both
parties to a transaction are less likely to reside
in the same economy. The conceptual and statistical implications of this should be clear. Second,
while data collection for the national accounts is
often systematized, at the regional level equivalent data may be nearly impossible to obtain. This
is so because record keeping at the regional level
is often virtually unknown, and, also, because of
disclosure problems. Most importantly, national accounts are designed to provide an analytical basis
for national decisionmaking purposes. Key tools of
national policy, notably fiscal and monetary policy,
are not found in the regional developer's tool kit.
Hence, in devising a system of accounts, the regional analyst has analytical objectives different
from those of his counterpart at the national level.

The first step, then, in devising a set of regional accounts is to consider carefully what the
analytical objectives of the accounts are to be.
In figuring out how to achieve these objectives
through the design of the accounts, the analyst
should consider questions such as the following:
How can the accounts reflect and help throw light
on elements of major analytical importance to development considerations? How can relevant ethnic,
sociocultural, administrative, and other substructures be reflected in the accounts? How can relationships with the rest of the world be usefully
but concisely examined? What meaningful balancing
devices can be employed? What types of data are
available, and how can these be organized and processed in order to maximize their analytical usefulness?

It is not a simple task to answer these questions. But once they have been fully considered
and responsibly answered, the job of devising the
regional accounts is essentially done.

SIMPLIFIED EXAMPLES OF REGIONAL ACCOUNTING

Imagine a region with the following ten characteristics.

1. All residents are farmers.

2. The total value of farm products for the year 19YY at local market prices is Mu. 20 million. (Mu. = monetary units.)

3. Farm families have reported that, on the average, they retain 25 percent of what they produce for their own use and sell the remainder.

4. There is an uninhabited marketplace in the region where all farmers sell their produce to merchants who come there for the purpose on traditional market days.

5. In this same marketplace, residents of the region purchase their household and farmyard goods from drygoods merchants who also come there for the purpose on traditional market days. There is no other expenditure outlet.

6. Both the produce merchants and the drygoods merchants live outside the region. The produce merchants take all the produce they purchase with them for resale outside the region. The drygoods merchants bring all their wares with them when they come to market, and they take what remains, along with their earnings, when they leave the region at the close of market days.

7. Of residents' purchases at the marketplace, 10 percent is for replacement investment.

8. All transactions in the marketplace are for cash.

9. There are no personal savings.

10. The government neither spends nor collects taxes in the region.

If we follow the general rules and format of <u>national income and product accounting</u>, a set of accounts for our region, Region Z, might be designed in accordance with the illustration in Figure 5. In this set of accounts, regional income measures have been highlighted on the left side.

Available data have informed us that farmers retain Mu. 5 million of their produce and sell Mu. 15 million in the marketplace. Their earnings of Mu. 15 million are then used to purchase goods in the marketplace. Capital replacement purchases comprise Mu. 1.5 million of these expenditures. Thus, on the right side of the accounts in Figure 5, Mu. 1.5 million is registered as gross private regional investment. The remainder of the Mu. 20 million went for personal consumption expenditures in one form or another. Of this amount, goods worth Mu. 15 million were imported, and these imports were offset by an equal amount of exports, so that net exports amounted to zero. Government expenditures were also zero. On the left side of the accounts in Figure 5, the estimate of capital consumption allowances was based on actual spending for replacement investment.

When we force the accounts into a simplified national accounting framework, a picture is provided that enables comparison with the nation, perhaps, but it is not particularly useful for the regional analyst. First of all, even this simplified national format contains an excessive amount of unnecessary detail that may contribute to obscuring the essential information. Second, the accounts provide no indication of the rather important fact that one quarter of farm production never enters the monetized economy. Then, one might conclude from the accounts that capital consumption allowances are calculated on the basis of refined business practices. In other words, the way in which

FIGURE 5

Income and Product Accounts for Region Z, 19YY
(Thousands of Monetary Units)

Regional Income and Other Charges Against Gross Regional Product		Gross Regional Product	
Personal savings	00	Personal consumption expenditures	18,500
Personal consumption expenditures	18,500		
Subtotal: Personal disposable income	18,500	Gross private regional investment	1,500
Personal taxes	00		
Subtotal: Personal income	18,500	Government expenditures	00
Transfer payments	(00)		
Undistributed profits	(00)		
Corporate income tax	(00)	Net exports	(00)
		Exports	15,000
Subtotal: Regional income	18,500	Imports	(15,000)
Indirect business taxes	00		
Subtotal: Net regional product	18,500		
Capital consumption allowances	1,500		
Gross regional product	20,000	Gross regional product	20,000

investment decisionmaking works (when a piece of
equipment breaks, the farmer strolls to the marketplace to buy a new part), is not reflected in the
accounts. In general, the accounts, as presented,
convey no real "feel" for the economy of the region.
Indeed, the accounts in Figure 5 provide no indication that the region is exclusively agricultural.

If we use the national framework as a starting
point, however, a set of accounts might be devised
along lines illustrated in Figure 6. Here, the explicit shortcomings of the previous set of accounts
have been overcome. The structure and operation of
the primitive farm economy stand out relatively
clearly. Even the "zero" entries have been thought
out and contribute useful information about the region.

But the social accounts are a highly flexible
tool. The analyst may choose to minimize detail
and emphasize a single aspect of the economy in
which he is interested or to which he wishes to
draw attention. The illustration in Figure 7 represents an approach to accounting for Region Z that
emphasizes sources of income and uses of product of
the region's residents. In this format, uses of income are not dealt with, and product is computed
directly by industry category (in this case, there
is only one), instead of through the summation of
the expenditure categories to which it is equal.

Or the analyst may prefer to use an accounting
framework other than income and product. In Figure
8, the data for Region Z have been organized according to expenditures of and purchases from residents
of the region. In this case, detail has again been
suppressed, and the analyst has emphasized the
import-export features of the economy.

All the illustrations so far are based on the
residence principle. That is, they are concerned
with the region in terms of the resident population
alone and not with the region as geographic space.

FIGURE 6

Income and Product Accounts for Region Z, 19YY
Modified Format
(Thousands of Monetary Units)

Gross Regional Income		Gross Regional Product	
Personal cash savings	00	Personal consumption expenditures:	
Cash income used for farm capital replacement purchases	1,500	Imputed value of produce consumed on the farm	5,000
		Cash purchases	13,500
Cash income available for purchases of household and farmyard consumption goods	13,500	Gross private regional investment:	
		Replacement investment	1,500
		Growth investment	00
Subtotal: Personal cash income 15,000			
		Government expenditures	00
Imputed income from sales of farm produce to self	5,000		
		Net exports	00
Income from nonfarm activities	00	Exports 15,000	
Income from all other sources	00	Imports (15,000)	
Taxes	00		
Gross regional income	20,000	Gross regional product	20,000

45

FIGURE 7

Residents' Income and Product, by Source and Use,
Region Z, 19YY, Simplified Format
(Thousands of Monetary Units)

Residents' Income		Residents' Product	
Income from exports	15,000	Value of farm products	20,000
		For export 15,000	
Imputed income from		For local	
sales of farm		consumption 5,000	
produce to self	5,000		
Total residents' income	20,000	Total residents' product	20,000

FIGURE 8

Expenditures of and Purchases from Residents,
by Origin, Region Z, 19YY, Simplified Format
(Thousands of Monetary Units)

Residents' Expenditures		Purchases from Residents	
Imports	15,000	By rest of world	15,000
Local goods	5,000	By local residents	5,000
Total expenditures of residents	20,000	Total purchases from residents *	20,000

They lose the locational import of the marketplace
which is geographically within the region but eco-
nomically outside it. This significant point might
be registered in the accounts, as in Figure 9, by
introducing the economic activity in the marketplace (to show that it is located in the region),
and then "adjusting" it out (to show that it is effectively outside the region).

If the region is viewed as a geographic unit
alone, Mu. 35 million of activity takes place. Accounts could be constructed on a geographic basis
alone, but this is generally not too meaningful.
It is usually meaningful and important, however, to
compare the economy of the region as a geographic
unit with the economy of the region as a population
unit. The simple import-export distinction may not
provide an adequate reflection of the spatial significance of what has transpired. Figures 5 through
8 could have been constructed in the same way if the
marketplace had been located outside the region. In
Figure 9, the basic data are the same, but information significant for the regional analyst that was
obscured in previous illustrations has been highlighted.

AN EXPANDED EXAMPLE OF REGIONAL ACCOUNTING

Figure 10 provides an illustration of regional
accounts that follows a format very different from
any of the previous illustrations. Here, the accounts are concerned only with personal income, particularly with personal income derived from earnings and that excludes property income and other income not derived from current production in the region.

Data on earnings have been collected at the
paying establishments rather than at the earning
households. Considerable detail on earnings is provided in a double-entry framework, first by type of
payments, and then by industry category.

FIGURE 9

Regional Income and Product, with Explicit Locational Adjustment,
Region Z, 19YY, Simplified Format
(Thousands of Monetary Units)

Regional Income		
Farm income		20,000
From imputed value of produce consumed on the farm	5,000	
From cash sales to exporting merchants	15,000	
Total income of region's residents		20,000

Regional Product		
Value of farm products		20,000
For home consumption	5,000	
For export	15,000	
Gross sales of merchants		15,000
Consumption goods	13,500	
Capital goods	1,500	
		35,000
(Less value of goods imported and earnings taken "abroad" by nonresident merchants)		(15,000)
Total product of region's residents		20,000

48

FIGURE 10

Income Accounts for Region Q, 19XX and 19YY
(Thousands of Constant Monetary Units)

	19XX	19YY
Earnings by type of payment		
Wages and salaries	650	1,750
Other labor income	15	50
Proprietors' income	110	200
Earnings by industry category		
Farm	425	575
Nonfarm	350	1,425
Government	35	250
Central	30	175
Civilian	30	100
Military	00	75
Local	5	75
Private nonfarm	315	1,175
Manufacturing	110	635
Mining	5	5
Construction	40	100
Communication & transportation	35	80
Trade	70	175
Finance & related services	20	45
Other services & utilities	30	125
Other	5	10
Total earnings paid by Region Q establishments	775	2,000
Residence adjustment	(10)	(295)
Total earnings of Region Q residents	765	1,705
Property income	75	260
Transfer payments	20	75
Less personal contributions to social insurance	(5)	(50)
Total personal income of Region Q residents	855	1,990
Population (thousands)	57.5	80.5
Percapita income (monetary units)	15.0	25.0
Index: national percapita income = 100	60.0	85.0

In order to convert earnings paid by establishments in the region into earnings of the region's
residents, a net residence adjustment is included.
The negative residence adjustment figures show that
the earnings of residents who commute to work in
the region exceed those of the region's residents
who commute to work outside the region. It would
be useful to have the residence adjustment disaggregated by inflows and outflows, by type of payment,
and by industry category. However, detailed data
of this sort are usually most difficult to obtain.
The residence adjustment is generally arrived at by
estimation techniques based on sample data that sel-
dome are adequate for disaggregated estimates.

Next, other types of income are added to total
earnings of residents, and other adjustments are
made in order to arrive at total personal income of
residents of the region.

As a useful addendum to the accounts, percapita
personal income is computed and indexed on national
percapita income for the two years.

If a similar set of accounts were supplied for
the nation or some other reference area, a very complete income picture of the region would be provided
in absolute and comparative terms.

The accounts provided in Figure 10 enable the
regional analyst to answer or suggest possible answers to a wide variety of questions of major importance to development planning and include the following: What changes have taken place in the economic structure of the region over the period? What
might have caused the basic structural changes?
What have been the changing relative roles of the
various types of income and the various types of
earnings? What change has taken place over the
period in earnings of residents as a proportion of
total earnings generated in the region? What change
has taken place over the period in the relationship
of percapita income to total earnings? How has the
region fared in percapita income terms, relative to
the nation?

It is not suggested that Figure 10 is the correct method of regional personal income accounting.
It is one of an endless variety of correct methods.
In some regions, for example, a breakdown of income
by cultural groups might be more meaningful than
earnings by type of payment.

In many cases, it may be advisable to construct
several different types of complementary accounts
and take advantage of the unique benefits that each
offers.

REFERENCES

1.   Conference on Regional Accounts, 1960,
Werner Hochwald, ed., Design of Regional Accounts,
Papers presented at the Conference, sponsored by
the Committee on Regional Accounts (Baltimore:
Johns Hopkins Press for Resources for the Future,
1961).

2.   Conference on Regional Accounts, 1962,
Werner Z. Hirsch, ed., Elements of Regional Accounts,
Papers presented at the Conference sponsored by the
Committee on Regional Accounts (Baltimore: Johns
Hopkins Press for Resources for the Future, 1964).

3.   Stanislaw Czamanski, Regional Income and
Product Accounts of North-Eastern Nova Scotia
(Halifax, Nova Scotia: Dalhousie University, In-
stitute of Public Affairs, 1968).

4.   John Friedmann and W. Alonso, eds., Regional Development and Planning (Cambridge: Massachusetts Institute of Technology Press, 1964).

5.   Werner Z. Hirsch, "Design and Use of Regional Accounts," American Economic Review, LII
(May, 1962), 365-73.

6.   Werner Z. Hirsch and Sidney Sonenblum,
Selecting Regional Information for Government Planning and Decision-Making (New York: Praeger Publishers, 1970).

7. Werner Hochwald, "Conceptual Issues of Regional Income Estimation," Regional Income, Studies in Income and Wealth, XXI, National Bureau of Economic Research (Princeton: Princeton University Press, 1957), pp. 9-26.

8. W. Hochwald et al., Local Impact of Foreign Trade: A Study in Methods of Local Economic Accounting (Washington, D.C.: National Planning Association, 1960).

9. Walter Isard, Methods of Regional Analysis: An Introduction to Regional Science (New York: Massachusetts Institute of Technology and Wiley, 1960).

10. George Jaszi et al., Readings in Concepts and Methods of National Income Statistics (Washington, D.C.: Office of Business Economics, U.S. Department of Commerce, 1970).

11. Charles L. Leven, "Regional and Interregional Accounts in Perspective," Regional Science Association Papers and Proceedings, XIII (1964), 127-44.

12. Charles L. Leven et al., An Analytical Framework for Regional Development Policy (Cambridge: Massachusetts Institute of Technology Press, 1970).

13. National Bureau of Economic Research, Regional Income, Studies in Income and Wealth, XXI (Princeton: Princeton University Press, 1957).

14. L. Needleman, ed., Regional Analysis (Harmondsworth, England: Penguin Books, 1968).

15. Richard Stone, "Social Accounts of the Regional Level: A Survey," in Walter Isard and John H. Cumberland, eds., Regional Economic Planning (Paris: Organization for European Economic Cooperation, 1961), pp. 263-93.

16. U.S. Department of Commerce, Office of Business Economics, National Income, A supplement to the Survey of Current Business (Washington, D.C.: U.S. Department of Commerce, 1954).

17. U.S. Department of Commerce, Office of Business Economics, U.S. Income and Output, A supplement to the Survey of Current Business (Washington, D.C.: U.S. Department of Commerce, 1958).

18. U.S. Department of Health, Education, and Welfare, Toward a Social Report (Washington, D.C.: U.S. Government Printing Office, 1969).

19. P. Wolff and P. E. Venekamp, "On a System of Regional Social Accounts for the City of Amsterdam," International Statistical Institute Bulletin, Vol. XXV, Pt. 4, 1957).

EXERCISES

1.   A regional analyst noted that the only new development in his region during the course of the year was the establishment of a new plant that employed 25 people at an average wage of Mu. 3,000 per year (Mu. = monetary units). Since this was the only change, he reasoned that the new level of regional income (an indicator of the new level of regional welfare) could be calculated by simply adding Mu. 75,000 to the prior year's regional income figure. The new percapita regional income figure could be calculated by simply adding 125 to the prior year's population figure (assuming that each worker brought with him the national average size family of five), and dividing this new population total into the new regional income total. Should the analyst be sent for more training, or should he be commended for devising a simple but reliable estimation technique? Why?

2.   In the period 19XX-YY, the following changes took place in annual-income indicators for a small rural region and for the country as a whole:

Income Increases	Region	Nation
Median household	Mu. 30	Mu. 320
Percapita	340	400
Median household percapita	115	110

What might have transpired over the period to bring these changes about?

3.   Figures 5 - 9 are based on imaginary Region Z with the following characteristics:

A.   All residents are farmers.

B.   The total value of farm products for the year 19YY, at local market prices, is Mu. 20 million.

C.   Farm families have reported, on the average, that they retain 25 percent of what they produce for their own use and sell the remainder.

D.   There is an uninhabited marketplace in the region where all farmers sell their produce to merchants who come there to buy on traditional market days.

E.   In this same marketplace, residents of the region purchase their household and farmyard goods from drygoods merchants who also come there for the purpose on traditional market days. There is no other expenditure outlet.

F.   Both the produce merchants and the drygoods merchants live outside the region. The produce merchants take all the produce they purchase with them for resale outside the region. The drygoods merchants bring all their wares with them when they come to market, and take what remains, along with their earnings, when they leave the region at the close of market days.

G.   Of residents' purchases at the marketplace, 10 percent is for replacement investment.

H.   All transactions in the marketplace are for cash.

I.   There are no personal savings.

J.   The government neither spends nor collects taxes in the region.

Devise a set of accounts that reflects this information, and then modify it where necessary to show the following changes in the region's characteristics (each change is to be considered separately):

A. The marketplace is outside the region instead of inside it.

B. One third of the farmers' purchases in the marketplace is for consumer nondurables, one third is for consumer durables, and one third (instead of ten percent) is for farmyard capital replacement goods.

C. Farmers store away 40 percent of what they retain for their own consumption and consume it the following year.

D. Of their revenues from sales of produce, farmers put an estimated Mu. 1 million in secret hiding places for use in emergencies.

E. The marketplace is once again located in the region. Drygoods merchants live in the region and manufacture their wares there from local materials. They purchase from each other Mu. 1 million less than the farmers purchase from them, and they also purchase from the farmers Mu. 1 million of produce that formerly was sold for export. Ten percent of the drygoods merchants' purchases from each other are for capital replacement. The produce merchants continue to live outside the region and to export the produce.

F. Add a lumbermill and a furniture factory to the region's economy (let your imagination supply the Mu. figures representing the types and volumes of their activities).

4. Consider Figure 10 and the discussion relating to it. Compute, for each of the two years, the percent of total earnings paid by Region Q establishments represented by each entry. Then compute the change over the period in the percent of the total represented by each entry. Finally, compute the percentage change in the value of each entry over the period.

For example, wages and salaries amounted to
Mu. 650 in 19XX and Mu. 1,750 in 19YY. This represents 84 percent of total earnings in 19XX and 88
percent of the total in 19YY. The change in percent
of the total over the period, then, was plus 4 percentage points, and the change in the Mu. value was
plus 169 percent. Numbers can be handled most easily
by simply drawing four more columns on the table and
filling in the computed figures for each entry.

Once this is done, answer the analytical questions posed in the text, namely the following:

A. What changes have taken place in the
economic structure over the period?

B. What might have caused the basic structural changes?

C. What have been the changing relative
roles of the various types of income and the various types of earnings?

D. What change has taken place over the
period in earnings of residents as a proportion of
total earnings generated in the region?

E. What change has taken place over the
period in the relationship of percapita income to
total earnings?

F. How has the region fared in percapita
income terms, relative to the nation?

4

LINKAGES, FLOWS, AND REGIONAL BALANCE-OF-PAYMENTS STUDIES

INTRODUCTION

There is a multitude of interregional linkages through which regions interact with each other. These interactions, in turn, generate impulses that work their way through the local, regional economy through an equally complex intraregional linkage system. The present chapter deals with several methods of examining interregional and intraregional linkages, both actual and potential, and the impact on the local economy, in balance-of-payments terms, of the region's interactions with the rest of the world.

Linkage studies are concerned with identifying potential flows. They seek to answer the question of how the region's actual or potential position within a set of interregional linkages can provide the bases for increasing the interregional and intraregional flows of goods and services to the benefit of the region's economy. This requires investigating several kinds of possible linkages, such as the following: (a) forward production linkages, involving further processing toward a finished product or expanding an existing production process so that a broader array of outputs are produced from the same kinds of materials presently used as inputs; (b) backward

production linkages that involve moving closer to
the basic inputs to a production process or even to
indirect inputs; (c) distribution linkages that ex-
ploit the region's location in the interregional
transportation network; (d) commercial and service
linkages that are oriented toward the region's potential retail trade and personal services trade
areas; (e) other linkages such as public service and
institutional linkages. In order to provide a point
of focus, the discussion in this chapter will con-
centrate on production linkages, but with a minimum
of imagination and inventiveness, the comments made
can be applied to other types of linkages as well.

Flow studies aim at measuring actual flows.
That is, they seek to provide the answer to the
question of how much of what flows where. The discussion in this chapter relates only to interregional flow studies, but the comments made can be
applied with a minimum of modification to studies
of intraregional flows as well.

The final section of this chapter is concerned
with balance-of-payments statements that also deal
with actual flows but are not concerned with identifying their origins and destinations. Balance-of-
payments statements seek to answer the question:
What is the money value of the flows that have taken
place during the accounting year between the region
and the rest of the world? One of the traditional
social accounts, balance-of-payments statements, often accompany regional income and product accounts.

Other methods of regional analysis that explore
the impact of the local economy of trade with the
rest of the world will be found among the following
chapters.

THREE SIMPLE LINKAGE
INVESTIGATION DEVICES

There is no single general tool to apply in
the investigation of linkage potentials. A few
rather sophisticated techniques have been developed

for use under certain conditions. Notable among
them is "industrial complex analysis." (See the
chapter on this subject in Isard, 1960.) But the
regional development practitioner to whom this book
is addressed will often find these impractical or
impracticable. Flow studies, balance-of-payments
statements, and methods of analysis discussed in
each of the following chapters of this book can
also provide clues to potential new linkages or the
potential expansion of existing ones. If the sole
objective, however, is a preliminary linkage investigation that can be performed easily, inexpensive-
ly, and quickly, simpler linkage investigation devices must be employed.

One such device is the linkage survey. This
is simply a survey of firms in various industry
categories in the region as well as in other selected regions (and especially neighboring regions).
It is conducted in order to uncover critical linkage aspects of the production process that might be
exploited for regional development.

The exact survey technique most suitable is a
matter for consideration in each particular case.
If we recall the analyst's concern with both forward and backward production linkages, the information required falls into two major categories, that
relating to outputs of the production process and
that relating to inputs.

For any production process being investigated,
the analyst would want to identify the outputs; determine how much, how, and where they are delivered;
what they are used for; if they are intermediate
goods, why they are not processed further; how the
selling of the output is conducted; and basic price
information. Inputs to the production process
should be identified by quantities and unit money
costs. Moreover, it must be determined where the
various inputs are obtained; how they are delivered;
what they are used for; how they are processed;
what substitutes are technologically acceptable;
and how the firm conducts the buying of these
inputs.

Of course, this does not represent all the
analyst would want to know about each production
process investigated, but it does provide the basis
for a set of lead questions for the survey. Representatives of firms will generally be hesitant about
revealing even this much information, and considerable inventiveness will therefore be required in
conducting the survey.

A less direct but in some cases more informative technique involves an <u>investigation of national input-output technologies</u>. If a national input-
output table is available, the forward and backward
linkages of industries on a national basis can be
studied for their relevance to the potential expansion of the economic base of the region. In the
absence of national input-output tables, linkages
of industries actually or potentially represented
in the region can be determined by interviewing
representatives of selected industries at the national level and by reviewing industry trade jour-
nals. Often it will be found that more valuable
linkage information can be obtained at the national
level because at this level a broader perspective
on industry input-output technologies is available
and also because at this level the industry repre-
sentative will generally have less fear of divulg-
ing trade secrets to the inquiring regional analyst.

Finally, the <u>location quotient</u> constitutes
what is perhaps the simplest of all devices for
providing at least a first indication of areas
where more detailed linkage investigations are warranted. The location quotient technique involves a
comparison of the extent to which selected economic
activities are found at the regional and national
levels, relative to other activities to which they
are linked. For example, the number of square meters of floorspace in cold-storage plants per hectare of vegetables and fruits grown by commercial
farmers might be calculated and compared at the regional and national levels. If the regional ratio
is lower than that for the nation, the possibility
of unexploited regional linkage potentials may be

hinted. In calculating the ratio at the regional level, the denominator (hectares of vegetables and fruits, in the above example) should encompass the potential service area of the region, and it should not be restricted or expanded simply to conform to the area defined by the given borders of the region.

There are a number of problems with the location quotient technique. In the first place, the analyst must know something about the production process before he can compute meaningful ratios. Then, the implicit assumption in using the location quotient is that what is found in the nation should and could be found in the region as well. It must also be remembered that the region is part of the nation, and therefore it influences the national ratio. These and other problems need not represent serious obstacles to the use of this technique in an exploratory capacity, however. Assistance from persons familiar with various production processes is available for identifying meaningful ratios to be computed, and where appropriate, norms other than the entire nation can be selected for comparison.

A fuller discussion of the location quotient appears in Chapter 5.

FLOW STUDIES

Commodity flows studies identify the commodities and their quantities that flow to and from the region by origin and destination. Usually, origins and destinations are given in terms of regions or cities. Information of this sort can highlight important interregional linkages, and in a more general sense, it can provide a commodity picture of the region's role in the national fabric. Time series information provided by flow studies conducted at regular intervals will provide insights into the shifts in import sources and export markets of the region and will give valuable clues to likely future developments. An analysis of data from flow

studies can provide a notion of the relative <u>dis-
tance frictions</u> of commodities exported by the region and clues to commodity and market combinations
with the greatest potential. Thus, commodity flows
studies provide data of immediate analytical value;
they also are of value in providing input to other
analysis techniques. In some cases, commodity flows
studies have provided the basis for balance-of-
payment statement estimates.

General commodity flows studies invariably
base annual estimates on sample surveys. Complete
counts may be possible only when the period of time
or number of commodities covered by the study is
very limited. Surveys can be conducted by <u>direct
counting techniques</u> at the borders of the region or
at delivery origin and destination points in the
region. Where a tradition of record keeping prevails, the survey can be conducted by <u>indirect
techniques</u>.

However conducted, the objective of the survey
is the gathering of information that enables the
construction of tables (matrixes) and maps showing
the origins and destinations of at least major
flows of specific commodities, by quantities. Figure 11 provides an illustration of a commodity-
flows matrix. The illustration should be considered as conceptual in nature because it is unlikely
that much could be gained by providing all the information indicated in Figure 11 in a single matrix.

More likely, commodity flows information would
be presented in a series of matrixes and maps that
could then provide greater detail in accordance
with what the analyst deems worthy of emphasis.
Greater or lesser detail may be provided by individual commodity; by commodity flows exceeding a
certain weight, count, or money volume; by points
of origin and destination; by flows exceeding or
less than a specified distance; by mode of delivery;
by a final or intermediate goods distinction; and
so on.

FIGURE 11

Illustrative Commodity-Flows Matrix

Commodity Flows to and from Region Z, by Mode, 19YY[a]
(Thousands of Monetary Units, FOB Value)

Commodities, Origin Region Z	Region X	Region Y	Big City A	Big City B	Total	Other Countries[b]
Cart: Commodity 1						
Commodity n						
Truck: Commodity 1						
Commodity n						
Train: Commodity 1						
Commodity n						
Boat: Commodity 1						
Commodity n						
Totals: Commodity 1						
Commodity n						
All Commodities						
Commodities, Destination Region Z						
[Use same format as above]						

[a]Estimates for 19YY based on surveys conducted Tuesday of first full week of each month.

[b]No overseas port in Region Z. Shipments to or from other countries also counted in region or city through which shipped.

Thus, the data from a general commodity flows
study might be presented first in a matrix that
listed the commodities or major commodities flowing
interregionally which originated in the region, by
point of destination, and those flowing into the
region, by point of origin. For each, the annual
volume of the flow by unit count, weight, or money
value would be indicated. This summary matrix could
be followed by others dealing in detail with commodity flows by mode of transportation, such as in
Figure 11; with commodities traveling over a specific distance (for example, only 50 kilometers);
with flows only between the region and the major
city; with commodities having flow volumes over a
certain weight (for example, 100,000 tons); or
other breakdowns that may be of special interest.

Conceptually, commodity flow studies present
little problem. In practice, however, their execution is not a simple matter. In the first place,
it will be found that obtaining complete information is a most difficult task, particularly in regions where large volumes of commodities flow
across the borders in individually owned rather
than commercial carriers. When surveys are conducted so that the annual estimates do not reflect seasonal irregularities, serious problems may occur in
terms of manpower availability and survey cost.
Then too, it may be nearly impossible in some cases
to distinguish between commodity flows terminating
in a particular region or city and those that are
only transferred to other carriers there. In general, as detail increases, so do the technical
problems.

For various categories of funds, money flows
studies provide the same type of origin and destination information that commodity flows studies
provide for commodities. Money flows studies can
complement and provide a crosscheck to commodity
flows studies. They can help point up financial
barriers to development, and they can provide valuable insights into interregional financial linkages
among institutions.

However, such studies tend to be of little value unless done in substantial detail. This detail requires a degree of monetization and level of record keeping not usually found in underdeveloped regions. For this and other reasons, money flows studies have often been found impracticable if not irrelevant for such regions. In most cases, special-purpose studies such as credit-source studies or type-of-savings studies will satisfy the needs of the analyst. Such studies must be devised in accordance with needs, institutional environment, and data availability in each case.

BALANCE-OF-PAYMENTS STATEMENTS

Balance-of-payments statements are valuable as complements to other studies, such as income and product accounts and flow studies, and also have substantial analytical value alone. They can provide, at a glance, a large quantity of flow information, and they enable analysis of the terms-of-trade and what has been called the net profitability of the region. The balance-of-payments statement provides the most comprehensive picture of the nature of the region's economic relations with the rest of the world. Balance-of-payments statements computed at regular intervals provide particularly useful time series data.

In compiling the balance-of-payments statement, the regional analyst is confronted with problems of disclosure, inadequate records, and the like, which are confronted as a matter of course in regional studies, as well as some problems unique to balance-of-payments studies.

Balance-of-payments statements are drawn up in terms of money. This means that the analyst may have to obtain unit prices for the goods that flow in interregional trade in order to estimate money values on the basis of unit or weight volume data from commodity flows studies or other sources. Meaningful prices may be difficult to obtain because different prices are often quoted to different buyers, prices may change during the year, and some prices are quoted free on board (FOB) while others are quoted with cost, insurance, and freight (CIF).

It is often tempting to base estimates on national average prices for the year, but this can lead to gross misrepresentation in terms of the values of the flows at the region's borders. Of course, the ideal solution to the problem is to obtain annual reports on the money value of goods flowing in interregional trade from exporting and importing agents in the region. However, this solution requires that the bulk of commodities and services in interregional trade be handled by a limited number of agents, that these agents can be identified, that they keep records satisfactory for the purpose of the study, and that they cooperate in providing the regional analyst with the information he requires.

There are other problems, particularly with regard to capital flows, but solutions are very case specific. Therefore, they will be left to the resourcefulness of the regional analyst to confront and deal with as appropriate in each individual case, with the help of the literature on the subject.

The objective of the balance-of-payments statement is to record the money value of inflows to and outflows from the region. The statement may deal with one or more specific types of flows, such as services or commodities, or it may record all flows. In the former case, its limited-coverage nature must be clearly indicated. The precise structure of the balance-of-payments statement, the level of detail, the way in which the double-entry balance is brought about, the way in which various substructures of the region are highlighted, and so on, are matters for consideration in each individual case, in light of analysis objectives, data availability, and the resources available to the regional analyst.

Ideally, in constructing the balance-of-payments statement, the analyst would want to be able to identify each interregional transaction. This would allow him to employ an inflow-outflow, double-entry accounting system based on the _goods flows_ principle. According to this principle, each movement of a commodity, service, debt paper, or cash is recorded in accordance with whether it is an inflow or an outflow. As Figure 12 illustrates, each interregional exchange would have both an inflow and an outflow aspect to it.

Let us turn to point D of Figure 12. If the region exported Mu. 500 of corn, this would be recorded as an outflow from the region by the goods-flows principle. And if, in exchange, the region received Mu. 100 in cash, a sewing machine, and an IOU for Mu. 200, these would be recorded as inflows to the region and would balance the outflow.

In practice, it is not possible to record each individual flow between the region and the rest of the world and the reason for which it was made. Indeed, it is not necessary to record or know this. Because earnings from exports pay for imports, conceptually, what really concerns the analyst is the net or balance of payments rather than each individual payment and the transaction to which it is attributed.

The traditional balance-of-payments statement uses the _payments-equivalent flows_ principle rather than the _goods-flows principle_. Under this principle, the net-payments figure is arrived at through a system that classifies each inflow or outflow in accordance with the direction of the flow of the payment to which it typically gives rise.

A common format used in regional balance-of-payments accounting is patterned after that used at the national level. This format contains four major headings:

1. _Current account_. The current account shows the money value of goods, services, and transfers

FIGURE 12

Illustrations of the Double-Entry, Goods-Flows Accounting Concept

A. Export of Mu. 500 of corn in exchange for cash

Inflows	Outflows
Cash (sales receipts) Mu. 500	Corn Mu. 500

B. Export of Mu. 500 of corn in barter exchange for sewing machine (based on market price of corn)

Inflows	Outflows
Sewing machine Mu. 500	Corn Mu. 500

C. Export of Mu. 500 of corn in exchange for promissory note

Inflows	Outflows
Short-term credit abroad Mu. 500	Corn Mu. 500

D. Export of Mu. 500 of corn in exchange for Mu. 100 cash, a sewing machine, and a promissory note of Mu. 200

Inflows	Outflows
Cash (sales receipts) Mu. 100	
Sewing machine Mu. 200	
Short-term credit abroad Mu. 200	Corn Mu. 500

and gifts flowing in and out of the region during
the period.

    2. <u>Capital account</u>. The capital account
shows long-term and short-term debt and equity purchased or sold during the current period. Capital
movements may balance a current account entry or a
cash movement.

    3. <u>Cash movements</u>. These refer to bank-
demand deposits and currency (and, traditionally,
gold) that move in or out of the region as the result of current account or capital account transactions.

    4. <u>Errors and omissions</u>. Records on inflows
and outflows are never complete, even at the national level. Thus, after careful, independent
computation of the current account, the capital account, and cash movements, any imbalance that remains is attributed to errors and omissions. However, it may be independently estimated or combined
with some other item computed as a residual.

    Figure 13 provides a schematic representation
of a regional balance-of-payments statement in a
modified version of the national format; three columns appear to the right of the item entries in
this figure. The first, entitled <u>exports and payments inflows</u>, records the money value of current
and capital movements that result in "new" money
flowing into the region. The second column, entitled <u>imports and payments outflows</u>, records the
money value of current and capital movements that
result in payments by the region to the rest of the
world. The third column provides the net balance
for each of the four categories, and, where desirable, for individual entry items. Thus, the inflow
and outflow represented by each individual interregional exchange are not recorded as such explicitly in the balance-of-payments statement. Instead,
all movements resulting in payments inflows are recorded separately, and all movements resulting in
payments outflows are recorded separately. If

FIGURE 13

Schematic Representation of Balance-of-Payments Statement*

Item	Exports and Payments Inflows (1)	Imports and Payments Outflows (2)	Net (3)
Current Account			
Commodities:			
Commodity 1 : : Commodity n	Money value of goods exported	Money value of goods imported	
Services:			
Tourism	Foreign tourist expenditures in region	Residents' spending abroad	
Transportation, financial, and other	Receipts from foreigners by local firms	Payments by residents to foreign firms	
Interest, dividends, other earnings, and transfers and gifts	Receipts from abroad by residents	Payments abroad by residents	
Totals on current account	Total (+)	Total (−)	Net balance (+ or −)
Capital Account Long term	Long-term commitments of residents to foreigners through foreign investment in the region, sales of equity and bonds abroad, etc.	Long-term commitments of foreigners to residents through residents' investment abroad, residents' purchases of equity and bonds abroad, etc.	
Short term	Short-term borrowings abroad	Short-term loans to foreigners	
Other			
Totals on capital account	Total (+)	Total (−)	Net balance (+ or −)
Cash Movements: Net movements of currency and demand deposits			(+ or −)
Errors and Omissions			(+ or −)

*Foreign and abroad refer to the rest of the world, including other regions of the country.

72

these do not balance, this will be reflected in cash movements.

The capital account and cash movements demonstrate how transactions on current account were financed. Thus, imbalance on current account must be offset by the net balance on capital account and net cash movements. Cash movements represent the residual imbalance from current account and capital account net balances.

In some underdeveloped regions, the capital account, or certain items in it, may be impracticable or irrelevant. In such cases, a revision of accounting procedures will be necessary. One possibility is to record values for those capital account items that are relevant and obtainable, and replace cash movements with a residual account entitled cash and debt residual, a procedure which is admittedly less complete and informative than would be desired. In the extreme case, accounting could be provided for current account only.

The example data of Figure 12 will aid in illustrating how the balance-of-payments statement format of Figure 13 would work. In the current account, the export of corn amounting to Mu. 500 would be entered in column 1, as if a money inflow had already taken place as a result of the export. An import of sewing machines of Mu. 200 value would also be entered in the current account, in column 2, as if there had been a money outflow in payment. Thus, the net balance on current account would be plus Mu. 300. In the capital account, opposite the item entry, short-term loans, Mu. 200 would appear in column 2 as if there had been a money outflow in order to purchase (import) the debt. Thus, the net balance on capital account would be minus Mu. 200. When the net balances on current account and capital account are added together, it is found that there remains plus Mu. 100 of the plus Mu. 300 imbalance on current account which is not covered by the net balance on capital account. Therefore, plus Mu. 100 must have been the net cash movement,

and would be entered as such in column 3. Figure
14 shows how the entries would appear.

FIGURE 14

Sample Entries for the
Balance-of-Payments Statement
(Monetary Units)

Item	Exports and Payments Inflows (1)	Imports and Payments Outflows (2)	Net (3)
Current account			
Corn	500	00	
Sewing machines	00	200	
Totals on current account	+500	-200	+300
Capital account			
Short-term loans		-200	
Totals on capital account		-200	-200
Cash movements (residual imbalance)			+100
Errors and omissions			00

The balance-of-payments statement based on
the payments-equivalent principle, as illustrated
in Figures 13 and 14, has an esthetic imperfection
in that the net column does not add to zero. This
is because the cash movement residual reflects the
net imbalance in the other accounts. Many analysts
have seen fit to overcome this by replacing cash
movements with cash outflow, with the result that
a net cash inflow takes on a negative sign.

In computing the accounts, many items may cause some confusion at first. In general, it can be determined whether a particular value belongs in column 1 or in column 2 by carefully considering whether the effect is equivalent to a payment inflow or a payment outflow. For example, the excess of taxes paid to the central government over central government expenditures in the region would be entered in column 2 because it is a net money outflow.

Finally, the point must be reemphasized that the balance-of-payments statement may be designed along lines deemed most suitable by the regional analyst in each particular case, as long as the basic accounting principles adopted are sound and are adhered to consistently. Indeed, the net exports entry in the income and product accounts can be viewed as a primitive and incomplete form of the balance-of-payments statement. The analyst can start with this and expand in stages to the full-fledged balance-of-payments statement as he succeeds in confirming the availability of the necessary and desirable data inputs.

REFERENCES

1.   Martin J. Beckmann, "City Hierarchies and the Distribution of City Size," Economic Development and Cultural Change, VI (1958), 243-48.

2.   F. Stuart Chapin, Jr., Urban Land Use Planning (Urbana: University of Illinois Press, 1965).

3.   Conference on Regional Accounts, 1960, Werner Hochwald, ed., Design of Regional Accounts, Papers presented at the Conference, sponsored by the Committee on Regional Accounts (Baltimore: Johns Hopkins Press for Resources for the Future, 1961).

4.   Conference on Regional Accounts, 1962, Werner Z. Hirsch, ed., Elements of Regional

Accounts, Papers presented at the Conference, sponsored by the Committee on Regional Accounts (Baltimore: Johns Hopkins Press for Resources for the Future, 1964).

5.   John Friedmann, ed., "Regional Development and Planning," special issue, Journal of the American Institute of Planners, XXX, 2 (May, 1964).

6.   John Friedmann and W. Alonso, eds., Regional Development and Planning (Cambridge: Massachusetts Institute of Technology Press, 1964).

7.   Werner Hochwald et al., Local Impact of Foreign Trade: A Study in Methods of Local Economic Accounting (Washington, D.C.: National Planning Association, 1960).

8.   Edgar M. Hoover, The Location of Economic Activity (New York: McGraw-Hill, 1948).

9.   Walter Isard, Location and Space Economy (New York: Massachusetts Institute of Technology and Wiley, 1956).

10.   Walter Isard, Methods of Regional Analysis: An Introduction to Regional Science (New York: Massachusetts Institute of Technology and Wiley, 1960).

11.   Walter Isard, "Regional Commodity Balances and Interregional Commodity Flows," American Economic Review, XLIII (May, 1953), 167-80.

12.   Walter Isard, Eugene W. Schooler, and Thomas Vietorisz, Industrial Complex Analysis and Regional Development: A Case Study of Refinery-Petrochemical-Synthetic-Fiber Complexes and Puerto Rico (Cambridge: Massachusetts Institute of Technology, 1959).

13.   L. Needleman, ed., Regional Analysis (Harmondsworth, England: Penguin Books, 1968).

14. Harvey S Perloff et al., Regions, Resources, and Economic Growth (Baltimore: Johns
Hopkins Press for Resources for the Future, 1960).

15. Allen K. Philbrick, "Areal Functional Organization in Regional Geography," Regional Science
Association Papers and Proceedings, III (1957),
87-98.

16. Robert H. Spiegelmann et al., Application
of Activity Analysis to Regional Development Plan-
ning: A Case Study of Economic Planning in Rural
South Central Kentucky, Technical Bulletin No. 1339
(Washington, D.C.: U.S. Department of Agriculture,
Economic Research Service, 1965).

17. F. B. J. Stilwell and B. D. Boatwright,
"A Method of Estimating Interregional Trade Flows,"
Regional and Urban Economics, I, 1 (May, 1971),
77-87.

18. Western Committee on Regional Economic
Analysis, Interregional Linkages (Berkeley: The
Committee, 1954).

EXERCISES

1. Construct a balance-of-payments statement for Region Z, based on the following information for 19YY.

A.   Records are extremely good because transactions are in a limited number of sectors only.   Errors and omissions, of course, cannot be known.   However, a study of historical data has shown that records in any year tend to err by 5 percent of current totals (verified by subsequent studies).

B.   Region Z exported Mu. 100,000 in cotton and Mu. 150,000 in rice in 19YY (Mu. = monetary units).

C.   There is a small consumer-goods industry in Region Z, which, in 19YY, supplied 10 percent of local consumer nondurable purchases of Mu. 50,000.   This amount comprised 50 percent of the industry's total sales.

D.   All capital goods (amounting to only Mu. 10,000 in 19YY) which were purchased by Region Z were of a primitive type and were manufactured locally.   Actually, most of the Mu. 10,000 is imputed value of homemade farm implements.

E.   There is no local-consumer durables industry, but all such products are sold through local agents.   These agents recorded sales of Mu. 75,000 at wholesale prices, in 19YY.   (They refused to reveal the amount of over-all mark-up on these goods.)

F.   Records show that the Mu. amounts for exported and imported goods (with the exception of consumer durables), do not reflect delivered price as they are derived from farm and factory price lists which are so-called factory-door prices (FOB factory).   The full CIF price is an average of 3 percent higher; insurance and freight are always

handled by firms local with respect to origin of
the goods. Consumer durables are excluded, because
for these, the price includes delivery by factory-
owned vehicles.

     G. Foreign ownership of farms and other
enterprises in Region Z received payments amounting
to 30 percent of gross export sales in 19YY.

     H. Rent and other income received by res-
idents of Region Z from property and debt owned
elsewhere was Mu. 3,000 in 19YY.

     I. Residents of Region Z spent Mu. 15,000
while touring other parts of the country for business and pleasure in 19YY, while nonresidents spent
Mu. 2,000 in Region Z for the same purposes in the
same year.

     J. Relatives of Region Z residents who
moved to metropolitan areas sent Mu. 25,000 to help
their families "back home" in 19YY. But Region Z
residents sent twice as much to relatives in regions where they were even more in need.

     K. The local government is confined by law
to an operating budget only. Thus, with no difficulty, it balances this budget perfectly every year.

     L. There were no private savings in 19YY,
and there seldom are in Region Z, except in the
form of the purchase of equity and debt from other
regions. In 19YY, Region Z residents purchased no
equity abroad, but they did purchase Mu. 5,000 in
bonds and Mu. 5,000 of short-term debt from residents and enterprises in other regions. No equity,
bonds, or loans were sold by residents of Region Z
to other regions in 19YY (nor to themselves, for
that matter, since no enterprises were created or
expanded, and household credit was available locally on an informal basis).

     M. The central government collected taxes
amounting to Mu. 40,000 from Region Z, and it

pumped back Mu. 15,000 in the form of infrastruc-
ture development and certain services in 19YY.

2. On the basis of the balance-of-payments
statement you have constructed for the exercise
above, as well as other information given above,
list some of the important observations you might
make, as a regional developer, concerning Region Z.
What sort of changes (in what items and in what
directions) would you hope to see over time as development progresses?

5

**RELATIVE
REGIONAL
INDUSTRIAL-COMPOSITION
ANALYSIS**

INTRODUCTION

For the regional developer, there are three
aspects to the term "industry location." (The word
"industry," as used here, should not be confused
with "manufacturing"; rather, it should be understood as equivalent to "branch of economic activity.")
The first deals with a determination of what was and
is the industrial composition of the region and what
is behind the past and potential changes in this
composition. The second deals with what was and is
the regional distribution of various industries and
what locational and other factors are behind the
changes in this distribution. The third deals with
all that is involved in bringing about the location
of particular industries in the region and in estimating and analyzing the impact of a new or expanding industry on the region's economy. These
three aspects of industry location coincide with
stages in the process of bringing new industries to
the region.

This chapter deals with methods for analyzing
the mix of industries located in the region relative
to the mix found elsewhere, particularly in the

nation as a whole. Thus, it is concerned with the
first of the three aspects of industry location although there is some overlap in the analytical methods that can be employed in each of the three. Mix-
and-share, location-quotient, and related techniques
provide means of understanding the industrial composition of the region, evaluating it in relative
terms, and identifying possibilities for the expansion of various industries in the region, all from
the region's point of view. Mix-and-share analysis
emphasizes the changes that have taken place in the
industrial composition of the region. The location
quotient provides a time- and money-saving shortcut
for gauging regional specialization and expansion
potentials.

For the regional developer whose main task is
the encouragement of new industry in the region,
the material to be presented will be but a beginning.
Performing such a task requires proficiency in such
additional subjects as linkage studies; plant-
location factors and the "locational process" from
the firm's point of view; feasibility, comparative
cost, and industrial-complex studies; methods of
estimation and analysis of direct, indirect, induced,
long term, short term, fiscal, and other impacts of
new or expanding industries; types and roles of
industrial-development agencies; techniques of pro-
moting industrial development; theories concerning
the role of industrial development in regional
growth; theories concerning the causes and natures
of interregional shifts in various industries; and
more. The reader interested in pursuing this subject can obtain considerable help from materials
listed in the References at the end of this chapter
and from the Bibliography.

MIX-AND-SHARE ANALYSIS

The change in regional employment relative to
the change in national employment over a period can
be viewed as the net of three "effects." The first
reflects the impact on the region of the change in

total employment nationally. The second effect
stems from the industry mix in the region, that is,
the distribution of regional employment among higher-
and lower-growth industries, relative to the industry mix prevailing nationally. The third effect relates to changing regional shares of total national
employment in each industry. The notions of industry mix and regional shares are compared with the
help of a diagram in Figure 15.

Mix-and-share analysis provides a descriptive
explanation of the change in regional employment
over a period. It does this by isolating the individual components of change reflecting the national-
growth effect, the industry-mix effect, and the
regional-shares effect. The formula, $R = N + M + S$
(where R is the total change in regional employment,
and N, M, and S are the individual components of
change reflecting the national growth, industry mix,
and regional-shares effect, respectively), provides
the basis for mix-and-share analysis.

Suppose the changes in employment in a nation
and in one of its regions, Region Z, over the period
19XX-YY, are represented by the data in Figure 16.
Total employment in the nation grew by 50 percent
over the period, while total employment in Region Z
grew by only 21 percent, less than half the national
rate. How can the difference be explained?

By how much would regional employment have
grown had each of its industries, and, therefore,
the regional total, grown at the same rate as employment nationally? Figure 17 shows the individual
industry and total computations for N, the national-
growth effect. Column 2 shows that when regional
employment in each industry in the base year is multiplied by the national rate of growth (which is the
same as the average rate of growth among industries
nationally) over the period, it is found that
130,000 new jobs in Region Z can be attributed to a
regional reflection of growth in national employment.

FIGURE 15

Diagrammatic Representation of Mix-and-Share Concepts

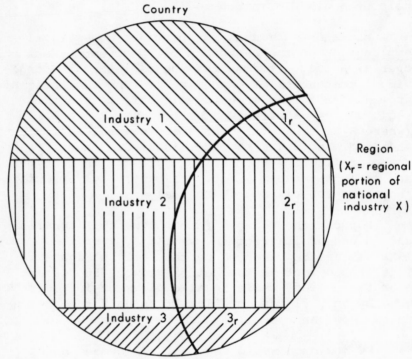

Country

Industry 1

1_r

Industry 2

2_r

Industry 3

3_r

Region

(X_r = regional portion of national industry X)

Industry Mix

$$\frac{1_r}{1_r+2_r+3_r}, \frac{2_r}{1_r+2_r+3_r}, \frac{3_r}{1_r+2_r+3_r}$$

relative to

$$\frac{1}{1+2+3}, \frac{2}{1+2+3}, \frac{3}{1+2+3}$$

Regional Shares

$$\frac{1_r}{1}, \frac{2_r}{2}, \frac{3_r}{3}$$ at the start of the period,

relative to

$$\frac{1_r}{1}, \frac{2_r}{2}, \frac{3_r}{3}$$ at the end of the period

FIGURE 16

Hypothetical Changes in National and Regional
Employment, 19XX-YY
(Absolute Numbers in Thousands)

Industry	Employment		Employment Change, 19XX-YY	
	19XX	19YY	Absolute	Percent
	(1)	(2)	(3)	(4)
Nation				
Agriculture	10,000	10,000	000	00
Manufacturing	5,000	10,000	+ 5,000	+100
Services	6,000	9,000	+ 3,000	+ 50
Government	3,000	7,000	+ 4,000	+133
Total Nation	24,000	36,000	+12,000	+ 50
Region Z				
Agriculture	150	120	-30	- 20
Manufacturing	50	80	+30	+ 60
Services	50	95	+45	+ 90
Government	10	20	+10	+100
Total Region Z	260	315	+55	+ 21

FIGURE 17

National Growth Effect, Region Z, 19XX-YY
(All Figures in Thousands)

Industry	Employment 19XX	N = Column 1 x National Growth Rate (0.50)	R = Actual Growth	R - N = M + S = Net Relative Change to Be Accounted for
	(1)	(2)	(3)	(4)
Agriculture	150	+ 75	-30	-105
Manufacturing	50	+ 25	+30	+ 5
Services	50	+ 25	+45	+ 20
Government	10	+ 5	+10	+ 5
Total Region Z	260	+130	+55	- 75

But actual growth in Region Z amounted to only 55,000 new jobs over the period. Hence, something transpired in the regional economy to offset the national-growth effect by 75,000 jobs. Since $R = N + M + S$, then $M + S = R - N$. Thus, the <u>net relative change</u> of minus 75,000 jobs by which the region "grew more slowly" than the nation can be accounted for by the industry mix and regional-share effects.

What was the industry-mix effect? To what extent is the regional deviation from the national-growth rate attributable to a regional, industrial composition weighted, more than the nation, by industries with growth rates below the national average? Figure 18 supplies the answer. The numbers in column 3 represent the individual, industry deviations from the national growth rate. The deviations were computed by subtracting the national growth rate (in this case, 50 percent), from industry growth rates in the upper half of column 4 of Figure 16, the original data. These deviations are then multiplied by regional employment in the respective industries in the base year. In this way, regional employment in each industry in the base year is "weighted" by individual, national, industry deviations from the national (average) growth rate. The results of these computations, column 5 of Figure 18, represent the regional, industry-mix effect.

Figure 18 shows that the industry-mix effect was negative in the case of Region Z. Columns 1 and 2 confirm that in the base year the industry with a rate of growth below the national average, agriculture, represented a higher proportion of total employment in the region than in the nation. The other industries, which grew at rates equal to or greater than the average, represented smaller proportions of total employment in the region than in the nation. The result was a negative industry-mix effect that offset the national-growth effect by 42,000 jobs.

FIGURE 18

Industry Mix Effect, Region Z, 19XX-YY
(Absolute Numbers in Thousands)

Industry	Distribution of Total 19XX Employment Nation (1)	Region (2)	Deviation: Industry Growth Rate Minus National Growth Rate (3)	Employment 19XX (4)	M = Column 3 x Column 4 (5)
Agriculture	42%	58%	-50%	150	-75
Manufacturing	21	19	+50	50	+25
Services	25	19	0	50	00
Government	12	4	+83	10	+ 8
Total	100%	100%	0%	260	-42

The regional-shares effect remains to be computed for Region Z. Since R = N + M + S, the regional-shares effect can be calculated residually as S = R - N - M, or 55 - 130 - (-42) = -33. In other words, the regional-shares effect can be computed as that part of the net, relative change (in this case, minus 75,000 jobs), which was not accounted for by the industry-mix effect. This residual can be computed for each industry separately.

If each entry in the lower half of column 1 of Figure 16 is divided by its counterpart in the upper half, and if the same is then done for column 2 of Figure 16, a comparison of the results will confirm the regional-shares effect computations. It will be found that regional shares of agriculture, manufacturing, and government declined in Region Z between 19XX and 19YY. Only in the case of the services industry did the regional proportion of total, national employment increase.

Summary mix-and-share data can be presented in a table such as Figure 19. The table presents the data in terms of absolute numbers only, but columns 3 through 6 could be presented in terms of percentages as well.

The analyst who compiled Figure 19 and the previous tables might have provided an explanatory analysis of the agricultural sector in Region Z for the period 19XX-YY as follows: Had the national agricultural sector grown at the national-growth rate, and had regional employment in agriculture reflected this same growth rate, the number of jobs in agriculture in Region Z would have grown by 75,000, from 150,000 in 19XX, to 225,000 in 19YY. Instead, however, regional employment in agriculture declined by 30,000 jobs, to 120,000 in 19YY. The gap between 225,000 and actual employment of 120,000 in 19YY, a net, relative change of minus 105,000 jobs over the period in Region Z, can be accounted for by two factors. First, the national agricultural sector grew by much less than the national average of 50 percent; indeed, it did not

FIGURE 19

Employment and Components of Employment Change,
Region Z, 19XX-YY

(Thousands of Persons Employed)

Industry	Employment			Components of Employment Change		
	19XX	19YY	R Change 19XX-YY	N National Growth Effect	M Industry Mix Effect	S Regional Shares Effect
	(1)	(2)	(3)	(4)	(5)	(6)
Agriculture	150	120	-30	+ 75	-75	-30
Manufacturing	50	80	+30	+ 25	+25	-20
Services	50	95	+45	+ 25	00	+20
Government	10	20	+10	+ 5	+ 8	- 3
Total	260	315	+55	+130	-42	-33

90

grow at all. Because it "grew more slowly" than
the national average, agricultural employment de-
creased as a proportion of the national total. A
larger proportion of the region's total employment
was in agriculture than was the case nationally.
Thus, the relative decline experienced by this industry nationally affected the region more severely
than the nation and was responsible for a relative
loss of 75,000 jobs. Second, during the period
19XX-YY, the region's share of employment in agriculture nationally declined. This decline expressed
itself as a relative decrease of 30,000 jobs in Region Z. Hence, the net impact of industry mix and
regional-share effects offset the national growth
effect of plus 75,000 jobs by a net, relative change
of minus 105,000 jobs; the region therefore experienced a decline of 30,000 in agricultural employment.

Analyses along similar lines can be provided
for each of the other industries and for total employment in the region.

In the above illustration of mix-and-share
analysis, the regional economy was divided into
four industry categories, and employment data that
covered a single period were used. However, this
represents the mix-and-share analysis technique in
its most limited and therefore least instructive
form. The analysis can be performed as well for
subregions and towns in the study region. In certain cases, it may be appropriate to employ a reference area other than the nation, such as a "parent"
region, state, or province of which the study region
is a part. The industries into which the economy is
divided for purposes of the analysis may be as disaggregated as available data permit, even to the
level of individual crops or products, and all industries need not be at the same level of disaggregation. (In the Region Z illustration, for example,
the analyst might have included a breakdown of agriculture by major crops.) The analysis can be performed for several historical periods, and it will
always yield greater insights when performed for
several shorter periods rather than for a single,

longer, time span. Employment is most often used
as the unit of measure because it is generally the
most available in a form suitable for mix-and-share
analysis. For certain purposes, however, value
added, gross revenues, sales, or some other output
or earnings measure can be used instead of employment. When a money measure is used in addition to
employment, the analysis may provide insights into
relative-productivity impacts.

    The mix-and-share technique can contribute to
regional analysis in many ways. It points up with
great clarity those industries for which further,
detailed study is essential. Mix-and-share analysis
provides an over-all picture of the role that the
region has been playing in the national, industrial
complex, and, in combination with other studies, it
is a powerful tool for pinpointing relationships between the growth of the region's industries and
over-all national growth. If national projections
by industry are available, the tendencies uncovered
through mix-and-share analysis can aid in using
these as a basis for projections of regional industries. Mix-and-share analysis can provide insights
into the factors behind observed changes in the region's population and in other growth indicators.
In helping the analyst understand the forces that
brought the region to its present state, and therefore where it is likely to go from this state, mix-
and-share analysis can provide a basis for preliminary development policy decisions regarding the region's industrial composition.

    Mix-and-share analysis may raise more questions
than it answers. This follows, among other things,
from its ability to focus on only a single variable
at a time. For instance, in the Region Z illustration, the analysis concentrated on employment,
while value added, investment, public spending, and
other factors that critically related to the region's industrial composition were ignored. In
fact, the use of employment as the unit of measure
results in a systematic understatement of the over-
all growth impact of industries undergoing the most

rapid labor-productivity gains. Furthermore, the
analysis does not explicitly account for unemployment, and it remains for the analyst to relate data
on changes in unemployment to the findings of the
mix-and-share analysis. As in all analysis models,
the source and quality of data used, the choice of
base and terminal years, and the level of industry
aggregation all seriously influence the results.

Finally, it must be reemphasized that mix-and-
share analysis is a descriptive tool only. As such,
it does not explain why a particular industry mix
prevailed in the base year, why different industries
experienced different growth rates nationally, or
why changes in regional shares of industries took
place. Nor does it evaluate whether the changes
that took place were desirable or undesirable. It
will be noted, for example, that a regional decline
in share of an industry that is experiencing a relative decline nationally produces a double-negative
impact in terms of net, relative change. The
negative-employment impact, however, may imply a
shifting of workers from low- to high-growth industries that may be very desirable from the standpoint of long-term, continuing, regional growth.

Hence, mix-and-share analysis has the potential
to make a substantial contribution to over-all regional analysis and to regional development policy
decisionmaking. It is essential, however, that the
analyst remain mindful of its limitations when making the transition from statistical results to explanatory analysis.

THE LOCATION QUOTIENT

In its most common form, the location quotient
(LQ), is a device for gauging the _relative specialization of a region in selected industries_. The unit
of measure conventionally used is employment. Employment in a selected industry is related to a
reference variable, usually total employment, at

the regional and national levels. Then, the findings at the two levels are compared.

Employment in a selected industry is "related"
to total employment by means of a simple ratio computation, and the ratios at the regional and national
levels are "compared" by means of another ratio computation. Hence, the location quotient is simply a
ratio of ratios. Following are two alternative
formulas, arithmetic equivalents, for computation
of the location quotient.

$$\text{Location quotient} = \frac{\dfrac{X_r}{RV_r}}{\dfrac{X_n}{RV_n}} = \frac{X_r \text{ as a fraction of } RV_r}{X_n \text{ as a fraction of } RV_n}$$

or,

$$= \frac{\dfrac{X_r}{X_n}}{\dfrac{RV_r}{RV_n}} = \frac{X_r \text{ as a fraction of } X_n}{RV_r \text{ as a fraction of } RV_n}$$

where

X_r = employment in industry X in the region,

X_n = employment in industry X in the nation,

RV_r = reference-variable value for the region,

RV_n = reference-variable value for the nation.

An illustration of the computation of a location quotient is given in Figure 20 and uses data
for 19XX from Figure 16.

FIGURE 20

Illustration of Location-Quotient Computation
(in Thousands)

	Employment in Agriculture	Total Employment (Reference Variable)
Region Z	150	260
Nation	10,000	24,000

$$\text{Location quotient} = \frac{\frac{150}{260}}{\frac{10,000}{24,000}} = \frac{0.58}{0.42} = 1.38$$

The arithmetic nature of the location quotient leads to the following rules of location-quotient evaluation:

$LQ > 1$: If the location quotient is greater than 1, the region is more specialized than the nation in the study industry.

$LQ < 1$: If the location quotient is less than 1, the region is less specialized than the nation in the study industry.

$LQ = 1$: If the location quotient is equal to 1, the region and the nation specialize to an equal degree in the study industry.

From this, it follows that if a broad-based aggregate, such as total employment, is used as the reference variable, a regional export industry would be expected to have a location quotient greater than one. A regional import industry would be

expected to have a location quotient less than one.
A local service industry would be expected to have
a location quotient equal to one. If the analyst
finds that this is not the case, it should be of interest and importance to him to find out why.

The location quotient was presented above in
its simplest form. A time series of location quotients can be computed for relative-trend detection;
location quotients can be computed for subregions
and towns in the study region; and employment can
be considered at any level of disaggregation, down
to a specific crop or product, in accordance with
analysis needs and data availability. In some cases,
it may be appropriate to employ a reference area
other than the nation, such as a parent region or
province, a median or average of other regions, the
nation exclusive of the study region, or even a
group of linked nations.

The specialization variable (the X variable in
the formula) and the reference variable need not be
in the same terms. When the specialization variable
is employment in a selected industry, as is most
often the case, "total employment" is but one of
many possible reference variables that might be
chosen in accordance with the orientation of the
analysis. If, for example, the industry under study
is a service industry and the location quotient is
to be used as an indicator of adequacy of service,
the appropriate reference variable might be population. If the service is oriented to households
rather than individuals and the service characteristically has an inelastic demand, number of households might be the appropriate reference variable.
And if demand is elastic, median household income
might be the appropriate reference variable. When
the analysis is oriented toward productivity considerations, revenues, value-added, or unit-output measures could serve as reference variables. When
using the location quotient as a tool in linkage investigations, employment or output in a linked industry might be appropriate reference variables.

In fact, the location-quotient technique can be used to gauge relative specialization in any sense and by any units of measure deemed appropriate by the analyst. The specialization variable need not be employment. (Thus, locational quotients have been computed using movie-theater seats as the specialization variable and 1,000 persons as the reference variable.) In Chapter 4, an example of the location quotient was given in which "square meters of floor space in cold-storage plants" was the specialization variable, and "hectare of vegetables and fruits grown by commercial farmers" was the reference variable. Where it is desirable that the region reflect reference-area proportions, the location quotient can be set equal to one, and the equation can be solved for the desired value of the regional-specialization variable, the values for all other variables being given.

As indicated, the location quotient has a wide range of analytical values. In addition to those mentioned or obvious, the location quotient can help highlight regional, relative inefficiencies, can assist in focusing on potential import substitutes or products with export-expansion potential, and can provide an indication of industries for which further, detailed study is most warranted. The location quotient has been found useful within the framework of linkage analysis, economic base analysis, input-output analysis, mix-and-share analysis, and more. Because of its simplicity, the location quotient can be computed many times, relative to many reference variables, time periods, and reference areas, with a minimum investment in time, manpower, and money. In fact, this device has been found so handy that an entire family of related measures has been developed for various specialized purposes. An excellent introduction to these will be found in Chapter 7 of Isard (1960).

Unfortunately, the ease with which the location quotient is computed can lead to its overuse and to an overstatement of its significance. It is, at best, a rough, descriptive indicator. Results of location-quotient computations will be

seriously influenced by the level of disaggregation
of the specialization variables selected, the choice
of reference variables, the choice of reference
areas, and the choice of years for which it is computed. It will be found, too, that the location-
quotient computation produces results of inconsis-
tent significance for different industries. Furthermore, the caveats implicit in any interareal comparison apply as well to the location quotient. Interareal differences in tastes and needs, levels of income, family sizes, exploitable resources, labor
practices, and, therefore, economic structure, require that statistical results of location-quotient
computations receive cautious analytical interpretation.

REFERENCES

1. Lowell D. Ashby, "The Geographic Redistribution of Employment: An Examination of the Elements of Change," Survey of Current Business, XLVI,
10 (October, 1964), 13-20.

2. Charles W. Blowers, "Measuring Growth Patterns in Employment by County: A Critique," Tennessee Survey, II, 10 (June, 1967), 1-6, 14.

3. T. W. Buck, "Shift and Share Analysis--A
Guide to Regional Policy?" Regional Studies, IV, 4
(December, 1970), 445-50.

4. Edgar S. Dunn, Jr., "A Statistical and
Analytical Technique for Regional Analysis," Re-
gional Science Association Papers and Proceedings,
VI (1960), 97-112.

5. Victor Robert Fuchs, "Statistical Explanations of the Relative Shift of Manufacturing Among
Regions of the United States," Regional Science
Association Papers and Proceedings, VIII (1962),
105-26.

6. Melvin L. Greenhut, "An Explanation of Industrial Development in Underdeveloped Areas of the United States," Land Economics, XXXVI (November, 1960), 371-79.

7. Melvin L. Greenhut, Plant Location in Theory and in Practice: The Economics of Space (Chapel Hill: University of North Carolina Press, 1956).

8. Melvin L. Greenhut, "Size of Markets Versus Transportation Costs in Industrial Location Surveys and Theory," Journal of Industrial Economics, VIII (March, 1960), 172-84.

9. Edgar M. Hoover, The Location of Economic Activity (New York: McGraw-Hill, 1948).

10. David B. Houston, "The Shift and Share Analysis of Regional Growth: A Critique," The Southern Economic Journal, XXXIII, 4 (April, 1967), 577-81.

11. Walter Isard, Location and Space Economy (New York: Massachusetts Institute of Technology and Wiley, 1956).

12. Walter Isard, Methods of Regional Analysis: An Introduction to Regional Science (New York: Massachusetts Institute of Technology and Wiley, 1960).

13. August Lösch, The Economics of Location, translated from the second revised edition by W. H. Woglom (New Haven: Yale University Press, 1954).

14. Harvey S. Perloff and Vera W. Dodds, How a Region Grows: Area Development in the U.S. Economy (New York: Committee for Economic Development, 1963).

15. Harvey S. Perloff et al., Regions, Resources, and Economic Growth (Baltimore: Johns Hopkins Press for Resources for the Future, 1960).

16. F. B. J. Stilwell, "Further Thoughts on the Shift and Share Approach," Regional Studies, IV, 4 (December, 1970), 451-58.

17. F. B. J. Stilwell and B. D. Boatwright, "A Method of Estimating Iterregional Trade Flows," Regional and Urban Economics, I, 1 (May, 1971), 77-87.

18. U.S. Department of Commerce, Office of Business Economics, Growth Patterns in Employment by County, 1940-50 and 1950-60 (Washington, D.C.: U.S. Government Printing Office, 1966).

19. Upper Midwest Economic Study, James M. Henderson, Anne O. Krueger, et al., National Growth and Economic Change in the Upper Midwest, Final report of the study (Minneapolis: University of Minnesota Press, 1965).

EXERCISES

1. Suppose a feasibility study indicated that a canning factory could profitably be located in a certain region historically specializing in the growing of corn.

A. Briefly describe the kinds of income impacts the region can expect in the short run and in the long run through linkage effects (do not try to quantify).

B. Identify the types of income impacts that might be direct, indirect, and induced.

2. Complete the analysis of the mix-and-share example from the text. There remained to provide policy recommendations for agriculture, and to provide analysis and policy recommendations for manufacturing, services, government, and the total region.

What additional studies would you suggest for Region Z toward providing a basis for a regional-development strategy?

3. Perform a mix-and-share analysis based on the following information for three industries selected for special study because of their dominance in the region (be sure to provide analysis and policy recommendations based on the processed data).

Industry	Country		Region	
	Employment in Thousands			
	19XX	19YY	19XX	19YY
Food processing	10	15	10	12
Wood products	30	25	5	8
Tourist crafts	5	8	3	4
Total for study industries	45	48	18	24

4. Suppose the data in the previous exercise represent the entire manufacturing sector in the region but only 50 percent of the national manufacturing total, for both years.

A. What is the location quotient for the study industries as a whole and individually, for the region, for each year (total manufacturing employment is the reference variable)?

B. What is your analysis of the results?

C. What other reference variables might be employed to probe more deeply?

D. On the basis of the results, what detailed studies might you recommend?

6

INTRODUCTION TO ECONOMIC BASE
THEORY AND METHOD

The heart of economic base theory is the proposition that the rate and direction of growth of a region or a city is determined by its function as an exporter to the rest of the world.

Sales to the rest of the world may be in the form of goods and services, including labor, that flow out of the region. Or they may be in the form of expenditures by foreigners in the region on goods and services that are immobile, such as those connected with the geography, climate, historical significance, or relative location of the region. The export industries constitute the economic base of the region, and together they comprise the basic sector.

Employment and income in the basic sector are a function of exogenous demand, that is, foreign demand for the exports of the region. However, numerous supporting activities are necessary to service workers in basic industries (and their families). Of course, workers in the supporting

activities service themselves as well. The supporting activities, such as trade and personal services, together comprise the nonbasic sector.

Both sectors, then, are related to exogenous
demand, the basic sector directly and the nonbasic
sector indirectly, through the basic sector. If
exogenous demand for the exports of the region increases, the basic sector expands. This, in turn,
generates an expansion in the supporting activities
of the nonbasic sector. Economic base theory holds
that all activity can be classified as basic or
nonbasic, that is, basic employment (or income)
plus nonbasic employment (or income) equals total
employment (or income).

The ratio of basic employment (or income) to
nonbasic employment (or income) is called the base
ratio. If, in a particular region, for every basic
worker there are two nonbasic workers, the base
ratio would be 1:2. If the base ratio is 1:2, then
for every new job in the basic sector, two new jobs
will be created in the supporting activities of the
nonbasic sector. Similarly, for every decline of
one job in the exporting activities of the basic
sector, two jobs will go out of existence in the
nonbasic sector.

If the base ratio is 1:2, the base multiplier
is three, that is, when basic employment increases
by one, a total of three new jobs, including both
basic and nonbasic, will be created. By multiplying the change in the basic sector by the base multiplier, an estimate of the total impact on the regional economy that results from a change in demand
for basic goods can be computed.

The base multiplier may be computed by summing
the two components of the base ratio, when the basic component is set equal to one. A more meaningful (but arithmetically equivalent) formula for
computing the base multiplier, however, is the following:

$$\text{Base multiplier} = \frac{\text{total employment}}{\text{basic employment}}$$

The formula has been expressed in terms of employment, but it could as readily have been expressed in terms of income or some other money measure.

From the formula for the base multiplier follows the formula for using the base multiplier to estimate total employment, given basic employment:

$$\text{Total employment} = \\ \text{(base multiplier) x (basic employment)}$$

If only the change in employment (rather than the level of total employment) is of concern, essentially the same formula can be used:

$$\text{Change in total employment} = \\ \text{(base multiplier) x (change in basic employment)}$$

On the surface, the steps involved in an economic base study appear relatively simple. First, a unit of measure is chosen. Most commonly, employment is used because of its availability. Employment as a unit of measure also has the advantage of facilitating conversion of the results of an economic base study into population or household terms by means of a normative conversion ratio. If available, income or output are equally acceptable as units of measure for an economic base study, and, for certain purposes, are even superior to employment.

The next step is to identify the industries in the basic and service sectors. Then employment (or income or product) in each sector must be tabulated. Once this is done, the base ratio and base multiplier can be computed in the manner described earlier.

An economic base study can serve the regional analyst in many ways. Its findings can provide the

basis for making estimates to fill gaps in historical data when only partial information is available,
and they can assist in understanding past and current developments in the regional economy. The base
multiplier is useful for evaluating or estimating
the impact of an expanding or new industry in the
region, particularly if the multiplier has been
computed on an industry-by-industry basis. It can
also serve as the foundation for estimates of future demand essential to the work of physical, public service, private enterprise, economic, and
other planners, and as the basis for estimates of
basic jobs that must be created in order to reach
target levels of total regional employment. The
base ratio and base multiplier can provide valuable
insights into the nature of the regional economy
through interareal and intertemporal comparison.

OPERATIONAL CONSIDERATIONS FOR AN
ECONOMIC BASE STUDY

The first problem that confronts the regional
analyst who sets out to perform an economic base
study is the selection of a _unit of measure_. The
two most common units of measure employed in economic base studies are employment and income.

As mentioned above, _employment_ is generally
the most available unit of measure, and it is easily
converted into other terms, such as population and
households. But in using employment as the unit of
measure, numerous, troublesome problems are confronted, such as the conversion of part-time and
seasonal employment into equivalent full-time annual employment. The analyst will also have to deal
with the problem of commutation, that is, residents
of the study region who work beyond its borders and
residents of neighboring regions who daily commute
to jobs in the region must be sorted out and accounted for appropriately. Because of these and
other factors, such as productivity, employment may
be a relatively insensitive measure of change, especially in the short run. The problems involved
in using employment as a unit of measure can be

overcome, for the most part, by careful application
of conventional, statistical and survey techniques.
Nevertheless, they introduce an added complexity to
the economic base study and make the findings subject to less than unique interpretation.

Income that accrues to residents of the region
may provide a more meaningful unit of measure, especially when the economic base study is being used
to gauge potential impact on the region as a market.
Some would argue that income also provides a more
meaningful measure of changes in individual and
community welfare than does employment. However,
problems of data availability and reliability often
preclude the use of income as a unit of measure in
economic base studies, especially in underdeveloped
regions. To be useful for economic base study purposes, income data would have to be available by
disaggregated sources. To the extent that such
data are available, they are often estimates based
on key indicators; reliability is often lowest for
rural development regions.

Naturally, the value of the economic base
study is enhanced when performed with the use of
more than a single unit of measure and the results
under each unit of measure are compared.

After a unit of measure has been selected, the
analyst next must consider a method for determining
which industries are basic and which are nonbasic.
A direct method of sectoral determination, such as
a survey in which firms and households in the region are asked to identify basic and service employment or income, would appear to yield the most
precise information. Unfortunately, however, direct methods require a high quantity and quality of
cooperation, and these can be very costly and time-
consuming. Consequently, they are often impracticable. Most analysts, therefore, employ one of a
variety of indirect methods for determining the basic and nonbasic components of the economy.

The simplest indirect method is the assumptions approach, in which it is assumed that all of

certain categories of economic activity are basic.
For example, a common assumption is that all manufacturing and agricultural production is for export
and that all remaining economic activity is supporting activity. In certain small and isolated communities, such assumptions can be made with reasonable
accuracy. In the majority of cases, however, many
industries will be found to have both basic and nonbasic components, and the economy will have an over-
all complexity that precludes such simplifying assumptions.

A second indirect method for estimating the
proportions of economic activity that are basic and
nonbasic, and one that seeks to identify the separate components within each industry, such as they
may be, is based on the formula for the location
quotient. The following formula derives directly
from the formula for the location quotient given in
Chapter 5:

$$X = \frac{\text{(national employment in industry x)} \times \text{(total regional employment)}}{\text{total national employment}}$$

The solution for X indicates the number of workers
that would be employed in industry x if regional employment in this industry relative to total regional
employment reflected national employment in this industry relative to total national employment. The
formula would, of course, work as well if income instead of employment were used as the unit of measure.

The location-quotient method holds that the extent to which regional employment in industry x exceeds X represents regional specialization which is
aimed at the export market, and therefore is the
part which constitutes basic employment in that industry. The total basic and service sectors can be
computed by applying the location-quotient formula
to every industry represented in the region. The
sum of the positive differences between actual and
X values is the total for the basic sector, and all
remaining employment is nonbasic.

Some analysts have employed variations of the location-quotient method that <u>tie the basic proportion of employment in an industry to the regional share of national population or income</u>. Under this variation, if regional population or income is 5 percent of the national total, for example, then it is assumed that all employment or income in a regional industry in excess of 5 percent of national employment or income in that industry results from production for export and may therefore be counted as basic. Industries known to be entirely basic or entirely nonbasic are not subjected to the estimation procedure.

Hoyt, in an article that appears in Pfouts, proposed a <u>combination of assumptions and location quotients</u>. He suggested the following rules of thumb to distinguish basic employment or income from that which is nonbasic:

1. All employment or income deriving from extractive industries is basic.

2. All employment or income deriving from "special" sources such as political, educational, institutional, resort, or amusement activities, is considered basic.

3. The basic proportion of employment or income deriving from manufacturing establishments with output not "intended predominantly for the local market," and in the remaining areas of economic activity, is determined by one of the varieties of the location-quotient method.

Methods based on the location quotient have come in for criticism from many analysts. The general shortcomings of the location quotient are summarized in Chapter 5. Particularly serious when used in economic base analysis is the failure of the location quotient to account for nonuniformity of demand and productivity throughout the country. Furthermore, the location-quotient method ignores the fact that a certain proportion of national

output is for foreign consumption. These and other
limitations of techniques based on the location
quotient can all be reasonably overcome, and a modified location quotient can be computed for each
industry, through sample survey and other research
techniques. However, at some point the research
required in order to enable the computation of a
meaningful location quotient may become so costly
and time-consuming that this method's chief advantage, its simplicity, is defeated.

Another indirect method in common use is the
minimum-requirements technique. This technique,
discussed by Tiebout (1962), involves the selection
of a large number of regions "similar" to the one
under study. For each such region, the percentage
distribution of total employment or income among
the various industries is computed. Then, for each
industry, the percentages attributed to it in the
various selected regions are ranked by order of
magnitude. A minimum-requirements profile, comprised of the lowest ranked value for each industry,
may then be drawn up that covers all the industries
represented in the study region.

The assumption underlying this approach is
that the region in which an industry represents the
smallest proportion of the total from among the selected regions contains the minimum requirement in
that industry necessary to service local needs.
From this, it follows that basic employment or income in the study region is the sum of employment
or income in excesses of the minimum-requirements
level in each industry. Because the regions selected for comparison may include some in which
truly unusual and irrelevant factors are at play,
the minimum-requirements level might be set at some
arbitrary rank other than the lowest for each industry, such as the third from the lowest.

Unfortunately, many problems accompany the
minimum-requirements technique as well. For example, how many communities represent a "fair" number
for purposes of comparison? How can the analyst

determine what constitutes a "similar" region in a
meaningful sense? How can the appropriate rank for
the minimum-requirements level in each industry be
determined? Often, these questions will receive
arbitrary answers. This is so because fully satisfactory answers would require, in part, the type of
information that would result from an economic base
study. Nevertheless, there will be many cases in
which a minimum-requirements approach will offer
the most practical basis for estimation of the basic and nonbasic components of the regional economy.

Finally, there is a host of problems concerning
classification of industries, or parts of them, and
the subsequent determination of the base ratio and
base multiplier, which may be unique to certain regions. These problems often arise in connection
with regions in which there is a large flow of workers across regional borders; in which there are industries producing a wide variety of products for a
wide variety of markets; in which a significant
amount of economic activity is in industries whose
products are not sold on the market; or in which
other unique features prevail. Commonly in these
situations, the only way to classify industries
correctly, apart from making rough estimates, is to
conduct surveys that will supply the necessary information.

A problem that the economic base analyst will
have to confront and one that is more of a conceptual nature is known as the time-lag problem. It
is recognized that the base multiplier does not
work instantaneously, that is, there is a time lag
between the response of the basic sector to a
change in exogenous demand and the response of the
nonbasic sector to the change in the basic sector.
The period of time required for the multiplier to
work itself through is not known, and for most
practical purposes it cannot be known.

A common approach to this problem is to ignore
it, on the assertion that over the long run, whatever time lag may exist is of insubstantial

consequence. Some regional analysts, especially
when performing an economic base study for projection rather than descriptive purposes, have tried
to make headway toward offsetting if not overcoming
the problem through the way in which they calculate
the base multiplier. Earlier, the formula for the
base multiplier, in terms of employment, was given
as follows:

$$\text{Base multiplier} = \frac{\text{total employment}}{\text{basic employment}}$$

However, some have suggested that the following
will give better results, in view of the time lag
problem:

$$\text{Base multiplier} = \frac{\text{change in total employment}}{\text{change in basic employment}}$$

Still other analysts have argued that if the base
multiplier is to be used as a projection device,
the time-lag difficulty will best be offset through
the computation of a historical time series of base
multipliers in which the latter formula is used
over a number of three-to-five-year periods. With
the time series as a point of departure, an estimate of the value of the base multiplier at some
point in the future becomes possible. A time series of base multipliers would also have descriptive, analytical value in respect to the past development of the region.

A convincing projection of the base multiplier
also would help overcome one of the major criti-
cisms of projection-oriented economic base studies,
one that stems from the problem of the changing
base ratio. In economic base analysis, estimates
of future impacts rest on present or past base ratios. However, successful development generally
brings with it radical structural change, particularly in the long run. And structural change in-
evitably expresses itself in a much altered base
ratio. Furthermore, one of the implicit objectives
of regional development is an increase in the

magnitude of the multiplier and a shortening of the
time lag, whatever it may be. Hence, the time lag
and changing base ratio problems are seen as particularly serious shortcomings when the base multiplier is used for projection purposes in development regions.

It should be clear from the operational considerations discussed above that the effectiveness
and usefulness of the economic base study increases,
generally, directly with the degree of isolation
and specialization of the study region, and in-
versely with its size.

In general, however, if executed carefully and
used cautiously, an economic base study can be a
highly useful tool for exploring, evaluating, and
(given estimated future basic demand) predicting
employment, income, population, investment, housing
needs, community-services needs, and other aspects
of the regional complex that are of major importance
to analysts and development planners. For an economic base study to be relevant, it is necessary
only that the economic base theory seem a reasonable explanation for the growth of the region.

THE TIEBOUT ECONOMIC BASE MODEL

The material in this section is based on
Tiebout (1962). While the material has received
some modification and reinterpretation by us, a
small portion of it has essentially been reproduced
from the original source.* The interested reader
can turn to the original source for a fuller expo-
sition of the subject.

The Tiebout model is presented in terms of income, and, as a matter of convenience, the same

---

*Permission to reproduce the material has been
generously granted by the publishers, the Committee
for Economic Development.

unit of measure is used here. Essentially nothing
in the following discussion would change, however,
were employment substituted for income as the unit
of measure.

Also, Tiebout's model is given in terms of the
change in the basic and nonbasic sectors, and in
the total, over some period of time. Again, the
discussion would remain essentially unchanged were
it in terms of total levels at the end of the period. If the reader substitutes "basic income at the
end of the period" for "change in basic income"
(over the period) in what follows, then he must
substitute "total income at the end of the period"
for "change in total income" (over the period); all
else remains the same.

We begin with the development of Tiebout's
simple economic base equation, which serves as the
foundation for the three-sector and seven-sector
models to follow. The following economic base formula was presented earlier, in terms of employment:

$$\text{Change in total income} = \text{base multiplier} \times \text{change in basic income}$$

To make what follows less cumbersome, the following
symbols will be substituted for words:

$$Yt = \text{total income}$$
$$Yb = \text{basic income}$$
$$Yn = \text{nonbasic income}$$
$$M = \text{base multiplier}$$
$$\Delta = \text{change in . . .}$$

(Economists like to use Y for income because
I usually means investment, and i often is
used for interest rate.)

When we use these symbols, the economic base formula given above can be written as follows:

$$\Delta Yt = M \cdot \Delta Yb$$

It is known from what has been mentioned earlier in this chapter that the base multiplier,

in terms of income, may be computed as follows:

$$\text{Base multiplier} = \frac{\text{total income}}{\text{basic income}}$$

The formula for the base multiplier can be written symbolically, and then, because total income is the sum of basic income and nonbasic income, it can be manipulated algebraically as follows:

$$M = \frac{Yt}{Yb} = \frac{1}{\frac{Yb}{Yt}} = \frac{1}{\frac{Yt - Yn}{Yt}} = \frac{1}{\frac{Yt}{Yt} - \frac{Yn}{Yt}} = \frac{1}{1 - \frac{Yn}{Yt}}$$

When we substitute the rightmost expression for the multiplier, the economic base equation can be written in the following manner with the use of symbols:

$$\Delta Yt = \left(\frac{1}{1 - \frac{Yn}{Yt}}\right) \cdot \Delta Yb$$

In words, the simple economic base equation would be written as follows:

$$\boxed{\text{Change in total income} = \left(\frac{1}{1 - \frac{\text{nonbasic income}}{\text{total income}}}\right) \times \text{change in basic income}}$$

The only difference between this and earlier forms in which the equation was presented is that now the formula for the multiplier has been incorporated explicitly. Readers with a background in economics may recognize the striking similarity between the formula for the economic base multiplier and the formula for the Keynesian multiplier, and indeed, the same sort of principle is behind both.

Given the simple economic base equation above, Tiebout's three-sector economic base model can now be explored. The three sectors of the regional economy in Tiebout's model are the export sector, the investment sector, and the consumption sector. Total regional income is the sum of income earned in each of the three sectors. In symbols, this can be expressed by the following formula:

$$Yt = E + Ir + Cr$$

where

E = income from the region's exports,
Ir = income from investment in the region,
Cr - income from consumption expenditures in the region.

From this it follows that

$$\Delta Yt = \Delta E + \Delta Ir + \Delta Cr.$$

The phrase "income from" refers to the fact that all spending in each of the three sectors does not result in local income, because some of it ultimately pays for imports, excise taxes, and the like. We are concerned only with that part of spending in each sector which becomes income in the region.

Income from regional consumption expenditures represents nonbasic income. Tiebout argues that basic income includes that from exports and from investment. The reason is that "basic," conceptually, should include those activities not directly dependent on the current level of income or economic activity. Demand for exports is obviously exogenous, and so the export sector is basic. However, investment in the region is also exogenous, since it reflects past decisions and future expectations, rather than a response to current activity, certainly in the short run. Hence:

$$Yb = E + Ir,$$

and in terms of change in the basic sector,

$$\Delta Yb = (\Delta E + \Delta Ir) = \Delta(E + Ir).$$

How does basic income generate nonbasic income in accordance with economic base theory? Income earned from exports and investment in the region is spent on local consumption. But not all income is spent in this way. Some is saved, some is spent outside the region, and some "leaks out" in other ways. Furthermore, not all regional consumption expenditures generate regional income. Some of the revenues from regional consumption expenditures pay for imports purchased from outlets in the region, some pay for indirect taxes, and so on.

If

PCr = proportion of total income that is spent on consumption in the region,

and

(PCr → Yr) = proportion of regional consumption expenditures that becomes income in the region,

then

$$Yn = Cr = Yt(PCr)(PCr \rightarrow Yr).$$

In words, income from nonbasic activities equals income from consumption expenditures in the region, equals (total income), times (the proportion of income spent on consumption in the region), times (the proportion of regional consumption expenditures that becomes regional income).

Earlier, the formula for the base multiplier was given as

$$M = \frac{1}{1 - \dfrac{Yn}{Yt}} .$$

When we substitute $Yt(PCr)(PCr \rightarrow Yr)$ for Yn, the multiplier formula becomes

$$M = \frac{1}{1 - \dfrac{Yt(PCr)(PCr \rightarrow Yr)}{Yt}} = \frac{1}{1 - (PCr)(PCr \rightarrow Yr)}.$$

When we recall that

$$\Delta Yb = \Delta(E + Ir),$$

we can substitute values in the simple economic base equation:

$$\Delta Yt = \left(\frac{1}{1 - \dfrac{Yn}{Yt}} \right) \cdot \Delta Yb,$$

so that it is expressed in terms of the three-sector model, as follows:

$$\boxed{\Delta Yt = \left(\frac{1}{1 - (PCr)(PCr \rightarrow Yr)} \right) \cdot \Delta(E + Ir)}$$

It can be seen that the denominator of the multiplier expression will have a value less than one. Therefore, the value of the multiplier will always be greater than one.

Suppose research based on sample surveys indicated that of each Mu. 1.00 of regional income, only Mu. 0.60 is spent on consumption in the region. And suppose it were also found that of every Mu. 1.00 spent on consumption in the region, only Mu. 0.50 became regional income, while the remaining Mu. 0.50 paid for goods imported for sale in the region. We can now compute the value of the multiplier in the three-sector model as follows:

$$PCr = \frac{3}{5},$$

$$(PCr \rightarrow Yr) = \frac{1}{2},$$

and the multiplier would be

$$M = \frac{1}{1 - \left(\frac{3}{5}\right)\left(\frac{1}{2}\right)} = \frac{1}{1 - \frac{3}{10}} = \frac{1}{\frac{7}{10}} = \frac{10}{7} = 1.43.$$

Therefore, in this case,

$$\Delta Yt = (1.43) \cdot \Delta(E + Ir).$$

The value of the multiplier in this example can be viewed as 1 + 0.43. Thus, the change in total regional income will equal the change in basic income (E + Ir), plus another 43 percent of the change in basic income. In other words, every additional Mu. 1.00 in basic income will generate an additional Mu. 0.43 in nonbasic (regional consumption) income. The base ratio is 1:0.43.

Now, values for changes in regional income from exports and investment can be estimated or hypothesized, and the resulting change in total regional income can be computed. Or, the development planner may establish a target level of total income, and solve for E + Ir to determine the increase in basic income necessary to bring about the target total.

The two basic sectors of the three-sector model can be disaggregated into six smaller sectors as follows:

Income from exports:

    Ep = income from private exports,
    Eg = income from exports to the central
         government.

Income from regional investment:

Irb = income from regional business
       investment,

Irh = income from regional housing
       investment,

Irg = income from government investment
       in the region,

COrg = income from current operations of
        government in the region.

These, together with the nonbasic sector (consumption) comprise the seven sectors of Tiebout's
expanded model. Simply a disaggregated version of
the previous three-sector model, the <u>seven-sector
short run model</u> may be written, in symbols:

$$\Delta Yt = \left(\frac{1}{1 - (PCr)(PCr \rightarrow Yr)}\right) \cdot \Delta(Ep + Eg + Irb + Irh + Irg + COrg).$$

Tiebout argues that, in the longer run, only
the export sector is basic. In the long run, the
other sectors do not cause growth but are caused by
it. Thus, in the long run,

$$\Delta Yb = \Delta(Ep + Eg)$$

$$\Delta Yn = \Delta(Cr + Irb + Irh + Irg + COrg).$$

In computing the long-run multiplier, each
component of the nonbasic sector must be treated as
was consumption alone in the short run. When we
substitute the more conventional term "propensity"
for the expression "proportion of total income"
used previously, the formula for the long-run multiplier in the seven-sector model can be written
in words:

$$M = \cfrac{1}{\begin{aligned} 1 - [&(\text{propensity to consume in the region}) \times \\ &(\text{proportion of regional consumption} \\ &\text{that becomes regional income}) \\ + \; &(\text{propensity to invest in business in the} \\ &\text{region}) \times (\text{proportion of regional} \\ &\text{business investment that becomes} \\ &\text{regional income}) \\ + \; &(\text{propensity to invest in housing in the} \\ &\text{region}) \times (\text{proportion of regional} \\ &\text{investment in housing that becomes} \\ &\text{regional income}) \\ + \; &(\text{propensity for government investment in} \\ &\text{the region}) \times (\text{proportion of regional} \\ &\text{government investment that becomes} \\ &\text{regional income}) \\ + \; &(\text{propensity to spend in the region for} \\ &\text{government current operations}) \times \\ &(\text{proportion of regional government's} \\ &\text{current-operations expenditures that} \\ &\text{become regional income})]. \end{aligned}}$$

With these definitions of the long-run basic
sector and long-run multiplier, Tiebout's full
seven-sector long-run economic base model can be
written in symbols as follows:

$$\Delta Yt = \left(\cfrac{1}{\begin{aligned} 1 - [&(PCr)(PCr \rightarrow Yr) + (PIrb)(PIrb \rightarrow Yr) \\ + \; &(PIrh)(PIrh \rightarrow Yr) + (PIrg)(PIrg \rightarrow Yr) \\ + \; &(PCOrg)(PCOrg \rightarrow Yr)]. \end{aligned}} \right) \cdot \Delta(Ep + Eg)$$

The advantage in the disaggregation is that it
permits the analyst to consider each individual
source of basic income. However, the seven sectors
itemized by Tiebout may not be appropriate in many
cases. In some cases, further disaggregation may

be desirable; in some cases, less; and in some
cases, disaggregation into categories other than
those used by Tiebout may be appropriate. The number and definition of basic sectors are decisions
that the analyst must make in each individual case.
The important thing is to identify all sources of
income that are basic, that is, that are not a
function of the level of regional income, as appropriate in the short and long runs.

In considering the Tiebout model, the question
is likely to be asked: How long are the short and
long runs? There is no simple answer. They are as
long as intuition and research indicate they should
be. The short run, by definition, must be a period
over which all sectors, with the exception of those
classified as related to regional consumption, may
truly be considered exogenous.

Actually, the problem does not end there.
Many types of economic activity will have both basic and nonbasic components, and distinguishing between these remains problematic. For example, even
in the long run, private business investment cannot
be viewed as wholly nonbasic, especially investment
in export enterprises. Indeed, up to a point, exports may be a function of investment, not the
other way around. Ways will have to be found of
handling problems like this in a meaningful manner.

Solutions to many of the difficulties, operational and conceptual, that may be faced, are suggested by Tiebout (1962). On the whole, however,
the reader is urged to view the Tiebout model as a
case study, not of a technique but of an approach
to developing the technique that will be most suitable in any particular situation.

REFERENCES

1. Thomas Hammer, <u>The Estimation of Economic Base Multipliers</u>, RSRI Discussion Paper Series, No. 22 (Philadelphia: Regional Science Research Institute, 1968).

2. Walter Isard, <u>Methods of Regional Analysis: An Introduction to Regional Science</u> (New York: Massachusetts Institute of Technology and Wiley, 1960).

3. Harvey S. Perloff and Vera W. Dodds, <u>How a Region Grows: Area Development in the U.S. Economy</u> (New York: Committee for Economic Development, 1963).

4. Harvey S. Perloff <u>et al</u>., <u>Regions, Resources, and Economic Growth</u> (Baltimore: Johns Hopkins Press for Resources for the Future, 1960).

5. Ralph W. Pfouts, ed., <u>The Techniques of Urban Economic Analysis</u> (Trenton, N.J.: Chandler-Davis, 1960).

6. F. B. J. Stilwell and B. D. Boatwright, "A Method of Estimating Interregional Trade Flows," <u>Regional and Urban Economics</u>, I, 1 (May, 1971), 77-87.

7. Morgan D. Thomas, "The Economic Base and a Region's Economy," <u>Journal of the American Institute of Planners</u>, XXIII, 2 (1957).

8. Charles M. Tiebout, <u>The Community Economic Base Study</u>, Supplementary Paper No. 16 (New York: Committee for Economic Development, 1962).

9. Charles M. Tiebout, "Exports and Regional Economic Growth," <u>Journal of Political Economy</u>, LXIV (April, 1956).

10. Edward Ullman and Michael Dacey, "The Minimum Requirements Approach to the Urban Economic

Base," Regional Science Association Papers and Proceedings, VI (1960), 175-94.

    11.   Steven J. Weiss and Edwin C. Gooding,
"Estimation of Differential Employment Multipliers
in a Small Regional Economy," Land Economics, XLIV,
2 (May, 1968), 235-44.

EXERCISES

1. If you knew nothing more about a given region than that it had a very high base multiplier, what would you guess to be the situation with regard to its growth (assuming its basic industry is growing)? And with regard to its size and economic structure?

2. Suppose you are told that the region's high multiplier is based on employment, and you know that percapita income has barely increased over the past decade. What conclusions might you draw?

3. Given no other information, what might you speculate about the region in each of the following cases?

   A. The region has a high PCr, but it has a low PCr $\rightarrow$ Yr.

   B. The region has a low PCr, but it has a high PCr $\rightarrow$ Yr.

4. Use Tiebout's short-run and long-run seven-sector economic base models to estimate total employment in 19X1 and 19X9, given the following information for a hypothetical region:

Sector	Employment 19X0	Estimated Employment 19X1	19X9	Additional Jobs in Each Sector Resulting from Each New Job*
Private exports	3,000	4,000	7,000	–
Exports to the central government	200	400	1,000	–
Regional business investment	100	125	–	0.10
Regional housing investment	50	75	–	0.05
Regional government investment	15	20	–	0.03
Regional government's current operations	30	40	–	0.07
Regional consumption	285	–	–	0.10
*Determined by analysis of historical data.				

5. Use Tiebout's three-sector economic base model to estimate total income in 19X1 and 19X9, given the following information for an imaginary region:

Sector	Income 19X0	Estimated Income 19X1	Income 19X9	Propensity to Spend in the Region, by Sector*	Regional Income from Each Mu. 1.00 Spent in the Region*
Exports	100,000	110,000	150,000	–	–
Regional investment	3,000	3,500	–	0.08	1.00
Regional consumption	50,000	–	–	0.75	0.33
*Determined by analysis of historical data. Mu. = monetary unit.					

INTRODUCTION TO INPUT-OUTPUT APPROACH

The <u>total product</u> of the economy, by conventional accounting procedures, is the combined value of all the <u>final products</u> produced, or, <u>final sales</u>, during a year. <u>Total output</u>, by input-output accounting procedures, is the combined value of all sales that take place, or, <u>total sales</u>, during a year. The latter considerably exceeds the former because it includes <u>interindustry sales</u> of <u>intermediate products</u> sold (and resold) as inputs to production processes. Final sales are made in response to final demand, or demand for final products. Interindustry sales come about in the course of satisfying inputs requirements to the production processes that ultimately lead to final sales.

An "interindustry sale" represents a flow of goods or services between <u>processing industries</u> ("industry" should be taken to mean "economic branch"), expressed in money terms. Thus, while there is usually a "seller" and a "purchaser" in the common commercial sense, an interindustry transaction may be considered to have taken place even if these are absent. A transfer of goods

among factories under a single ownership may involve no direct payment, for example. Nevertheless,
it is considered an interindustry sale, complete
with a seller and a purchaser, in the input-output
sense. The same principle applies to "final sales."
Thus, even a transfer to inventory, which is "final"
in terms of the current period, is considered a final sale or delivery.

Input-output differs from other forms of social account, such as income and product accounting,
in that it deals with interindustry transactions
generated by the demand for final product. These
transactions represent the "double counting" that
must carefully be avoided under other accounting
procedures. The input-output model provides a
framework for arraying, processing, and analyzing
data in order to enable an understanding of the
interindustry structure of the economy and the implications of the unique structural interdependence
that prevails. Indeed, analysis based on the
input-output model is often called interindustry
analysis.

Input-output analysis divides the economy into
two major components, suppliers (or sellers) and
purchasers (or users). Each of these has two sub-
divisions, in accordance with the following scheme.

Suppliers include the following:

1. Intermediate, processing, or producing
suppliers are producers who must purchase inputs to
be processed into outputs which they sell as inputs
to other intermediate suppliers or to final users.

2. Primary suppliers are sellers whose output
is not directly dependent on purchased inputs. Consequently, payments to suppliers of primary inputs
are final payments, since, unlike payments to intermediate suppliers, they do not generate further
interindustry sales. Earnings of these suppliers
essentially represent value added.

Purchasers include the following:

1.   Intermediate, processing, or producing
purchasers buy the outputs of suppliers for use as
inputs for further processing.

2.   Final purchasers, or final demand, or final
users buy the outputs of suppliers in their final
form and for final use. The level of final demand
and its composition are determined exogenously
(outside the system). Production to satisfy final
demand generates intermediate purchases of inputs.

Intermediate suppliers and purchasers are one
and the same industries or sectors. Because of
this, the terms "industry" and "sector" are often
used interchangeably in input-output literature, as
they are in this chapter. Furthermore, their sales
and purchases are related to each other, since
their purchases of inputs are a function of the demand for their outputs.

Primary suppliers and final users may or may
not be one and the same. But in cases where they
are the same (households, for example, both supply
labor, a primary input, and purchase final consumption goods), their activities as primary suppliers
and as final users are taken as completely independent of each other, and they are treated as if they
were not the same.

THREE INPUT-OUTPUT TABLES

The input-output model consists of three
tables, as discussed below.

The transactions table contains basic data
concerning total flows of goods and services among
suppliers and users during the study year. The
flows are measured in (or converted to) money terms
and are viewed as sales transactions between sellers and purchasers.

The direct requirements table, derived from
the transactions table, shows the input purchases
required by each intermediate purchaser per unit of
output that it produces.

The total requirements table, derived from the
direct requirements table, shows the total purchases of direct and indirect inputs that are required throughout the economy per unit of output
delivered to final demand by any intermediate supplier.

The input-output model will be explained with
the help of a highly simplified example. Imagine
an isolated, island economy. There are no imports,
no exports, no government, no investment, no savings, no inventory. Thus, everything is purchased,
processed, sold, and consumed on the island, in the
current period; there is only one final purchaser,
households; there is only one primary supplier,
also households. Households supply primary inputs
such as labor and management. There are only two
processing industries, agriculture and manufacturing (really a collection of crafts industries).
Figure 21 is the transactions table compiled for
the island economy, based on reported sales during
the most recent accounting year.

The first row of data shows that of total
sales of Mu. 100,000, agriculture sold Mu. 10,000
of produce to itself for further processing (seed,
feed, fertilizers, etc.). It also sold Mu. 30,000
of produce to manufacturing for further processing
(industrial crops, foodstuffs for canning, etc.).
Mu. 60,000 of agricultural sales were sold to final
users for home consumption. The first column of
data shows that in order to produce the Mu. 100,000
of total output, agriculture had to purchase Mu.
10,000 in products from itself, Mu. 5,000 in manufacturing inputs, and Mu. 85,000 in primary inputs,
such as labor, from households. The manufacturing
row and column can be considered in a similar fashion.

FIGURE 21

A Simple Input-Output Transactions Table
(Thousands of Monetary Units)

Goods Sold by \ Goods Purchased by	Intermediate Uses — Agriculture	Intermediate Uses — Manufacturing	Final Uses — Households	Total Output
Processing suppliers — Agriculture	10	30	60	100
Processing suppliers — Manufacturing	5	10	35	50
Primary suppliers — Households	85	10	15	110
Total inputs	100	50	110	260

The rows, then, show the distribution of each supplier's sales to intermediate and final purchasers. The columns show the distribution of each purchaser's purchases from intermediate and primary suppliers. Naturally, for any processing industry, total inputs will equal total outputs. For the economy as a whole, total final demand will equal total primary inputs; this will correspond to the equality between product and income, respectively, by conventional accounting procedures. And of course, as the "southeast" box shows, total inputs into the system will equal total outputs of the system.

The transactions table provides a rather complete view of the interindustry flows of goods and services in the economy during the study year. It does not, however, constitute a generalized analytical tool. The question, then, is how to transform the basic transactions data into a generalized statement of direct input requirements per unit of output for each processing industry. The answer is, divide the inputs figures in each intermediate-uses column by the number at the bottom of the column, total inputs.

Since total inputs equal total outputs, dividing each intermediate-uses column through by the total will provide a distribution of inputs per unit of output for each processing supplier. Figure 22 shows the results of this simple computation, arranged in the format of a direct requirements table. The final-uses column has been dropped, because purchases by final users do not represent inputs for processing. The direct requirements table is often called the table of technical coefficients, because it shows the technical production-function relationships between output and inputs.

The direct requirements table provides the direct requirements coefficients necessary to calculate direct inputs required for any level of demand for the output of any processing industry. If, for example, demand for agriculture products is

FIGURE 22

A Simple Input-Output Direct
Requirements Table

(Direct Requirements Coefficients: Direct
Requirements per Unit of Final Delivery)

Output of / Requires Inputs from	Agriculture	Manufacturing
Agriculture	0.10	0.60
Manufacturing	0.05	0.20
Households	0.85	0.20
Total direct inputs	1.00	1.00

expected to amount to Mu. 50,000, Figure 22 shows
that satisfying this demand will require direct
processed inputs to agriculture of Mu. 5,000 in agricultural products and Mu. 2,500 in manufacturing
products. Also, Mu. 42,500 in primary inputs will
be required by agriculture from households. The
direct inputs requirements were computed by multiplying each coefficient in the agriculture column
by the expected demand of Mu. 50,000 for that industry's output.

In effect, every businessman or farmer has a
one-column direct requirements table for his business or farm, in his head if not on paper. He uses
it to adjust his orders for supplies in accordance
with the output he plans to deliver.

From the point of view of the entire economy, however, more than direct input requirements must be considered in analysis for planning. Direct inputs are only part of the total input requirements of the economy, because these direct inputs must also be produced, and their production will require additional inputs. Inputs of the latter type are called <u>indirect inputs</u>. But then, where do the indirect inputs come from? Producing them will require even more indirect inputs. And so, there emerges a pattern of successive "rounds," and the output of each round serves as inputs for the round that is one step closer to the final product.

The direct inputs are called the "first round" of input supplies. The first set of indirect inputs, those required to produce the direct inputs, are called the "second round" of input supplies. The next set of indirect inputs, those required to produce the "second round," are called the "third round." And so on. Calculation of total input requirements from the direct requirements table by the <u>iterative method</u> refers to the computation of all the rounds and the summing of the results.

To illustrate, we shall return to our island economy. Let us imagine that our island was suddenly "discovered" by a party of explorers. They inform us that, as they have already sent back word of their discovery, we can expect a substantial influx of population during the coming year. Of an enlightened breed, the explorers have brought with them estimates of the increase in final demand that will result from the influx of population. When these are added to existing levels, it is calculated that sales of agricultural products to final demand will amount to Mu. 200,000 and that Mu. 100,000 of manufacturing products will be demanded by final consumers.

The leaders of the island population are somewhat worried because they must plan to accommodate the expansion that will be required. To do this, they must know what the full impact of the higher level of final demand will be upon each sector. What is obviously needed is an input-output total requirements computation.

Figure 23 shows how total requirements might be computed from the direct requirements table. If agricultural sales to final demand are Mu. 200,000, multiplying this number through the agriculture column of the direct requirements table in Figure 22 shows that direct inputs of Mu. 20,000 are required from agriculture, Mu. 10,000 are required from manufacturing, and Mu. 170,000 are required from the primary suppliers, households. This computation is shown in the second row of Figure 23. In a similar fashion, the direct input requirements to enable manufacturing to satisfy the anticipated Mu. 100,000 of sales to final demand can be computed, as shown in the third row of Figure 23. To-total direct requirements necessary to satisfy the final demand for both agricultural and manufacturing products are shown in the fourth row of Figure 23.

Total direct inputs sales are then multiplied through their respective columns in the direct requirements table in order to arrive at second-round inputs required. The totals for the second round are, in turn, multiplied through the direct requirements table in order to arrive at third-round inputs required. This procedure can continue endlessly, but Figure 23 does not go beyond four iterations. After four rounds, the numbers are relatively small in this example, and it is a good guess that the error resulting from truncation will be minimal. Nevertheless, a plus sign has been added to the totals for indirect inputs in recognition of the fact that these totals represent slight underestimates.

The recapitulation at the bottom of Figure 23 shows that in order to satisfy the anticipated Mu. 300,000 combined final sales of agricultural and manufacturing products, total sales throughout the economy of much more than Mu. 300,000 will be

FIGURE 23

Illustrative Total Requirements Computation from
Direct Requirements Table
(Thousands of Monetary Units)

			By Agriculture	By Manufacturing	By Households
Sales to Final Demand			200	100	--
Sales as	To Agriculture		200 x 0.10 = 20	200 x 0.05 = 10	200 x 0.85 = 170
Direct	To Manufacturing		100 x 0.60 = 60	100 x 0.20 = 20	100 x 0.20 = 20
Inputs	Total		80	30	190
Sales as Indirect Inputs	Second Round	To Agriculture	80 x 0.10 = 8.00	80 x 0.05 = 4.00	80 x 0.85 = 68.00
		To Manufacturing	30 x 0.60 = 18.00	30 x 0.20 = 6.00	30 x 0.20 = 6.00
		Total	26.00	10.00	74.00
	Third Round	To Agriculture	26 x 0.10 = 2.60	26 x 0.05 = 1.30	26 x 0.85 = 22.10
		To Manufacturing	10 x 0.60 = 6.00	10 x 0.20 = 2.00	10 x 0.20 = 2.00
		Total	8.60	3.30	24.10
	Fourth Round	To Agriculture	8.6 x 0.10 = 0.86	8.6 x 0.05 = 0.43	8.6 x 0.85 = 7.31
		To Manufacturing	3.3 x 0.60 = 1.98	3.3 x 0.20 = 0.66	3.3 x 0.20 = 0.66
		Total	2.84	1.09	7.97
	Total indirect inputs		37.44+	14.39+	106.07+
			Recapitulation		
Sales of processed goods to final demand in the value of			200	100	--
Requires direct inputs of			80	30	190
And requires indirect inputs of			37+	14+	106+
Therefore, total sales will be			317+	144+	296+

required. Total sales of agricultural products
alone will amount to over Mu. 317,000; total sales
of manufacturing products will exceed Mu. 144,000;
and sales of primary inputs by households will total over Mu. 296,000. This is the information that
the island leadership needs in order to plan for
the necessary expansion.

A word is in order concerning the role of primary inputs in the computation in Figure 23. Because no inputs are required by primary suppliers,
payments for primary inputs in any round (or by final users) are "final payments" that do not reap-
pear in the next round. It will be noted, in Figure 23, that the combined total sales in each round
are smaller than the combined total sales in the
preceding round by the amount of sales by households
in the preceding round.

It was noted earlier that ultimately total
sales by primary suppliers must equal total final
sales, just as income equals product, by conventional accounting procedures. In Figure 23, combined final demand amounted to Mu. 300,000, but
through the iterative process, sales of primary inputs came to only Mu. 296,000. This is accounted
for by the fact that only four iterations were
worked through. The more rounds computed, the
closer the total primary inputs figure will come to
total final sales. The limit of the iterative
process would be reached and "actual" total sales
for all sectors attained when total sales by primary suppliers equaled total final sales. The gap
between these two figures after a selected number
of iterations provides an indication of the distance from actual totals.

The iterative method for computing total requirements seems to have worked well enough, and
had we continued with it for several more rounds,
even more precise results would have obtained. In
the example of the island economy, all processing
activities were aggregated into but two categories,
agriculture and manufacturing. In most developing

regions, however, the processing sectors, for purposes of input-output analysis, will number between
ten and fifty. It is easy to see, in a realistic
situation, that running through the iterations in
order to compute total requirements can be a rather
cumbersome procedure. This cumbersomeness can rise
to prohibitive dimensions when total requirements
computations are needed for a large number of alternative levels and compositions of final demand.
It would be useful to have a set of total requirements coefficients that would enable "solving"
readily for any estimated or hypothesized final demand.

Furthermore, for purposes of descriptive analysis, a generalized statement of structural interdependence in the economy is needed. A set of total requirements coefficients arranged in a tabular
format would constitute such a statement, in the
same way that the direct requirements table constitutes a generalized statement of direct technical
relationships.

A total requirements table can be computed
from the direct requirements table by applying the
iterative method for Mu. 1.00 in sales to final demand by each processing sector, in turn. Figure 24
provides information similar to the recapitulation
in Figure 23. It shows the results of total requirements computations for the island economy,
based on the direct requirements coefficients of
Figure 22. These results obtained after six iterations (not shown); they started with Mu. 1.00 of
delivery to final demand by agriculture only and
then repeated the entire process for Mu. 1.00 of
delivery to final demand by the manufacturing sector only.

In computing the total requirements coefficients in Figure 24, a small adjustment was made in
the iterative method. Because it is known that total sales by primary suppliers (households, in this
case), will be equal to final demand, total indirect
primary inputs were calculated residually as the

FIGURE 24

Results of Total Requirements Coefficients Computations
from Direct Requirements Table
(Monetary Units)

	Agriculture	Manufacturing	Households
Sales of processed goods to final demand in the value of	1.000	--	--
Requires direct inputs of	0.100	0.050	0.850
And requires indirect inputs of	0.055+	0.022+	0.150
Therefore, total sales will be	1.155+	0.072+	1.000
Sales of processed goods to final demand in the value of	--	1.000	--
Requires direct inputs of	0.600	0.200	0.200
And requires indirect inputs of	0.268+	0.103+	0.800
Therefore, total sales will be	0.868+	1.303+	1.000

difference between final sales (of one) and direct
primary inputs. Indeed, it is not really necessary
to compute the total requirements coefficient for
primary inputs at all, since it will always have a
value of one, the final demand value for which the
total requirements coefficient is always computed.

The total requirements coefficients for the
island economy shown in Figure 24 are arranged in
the format of a total requirements table in Figure
25.

FIGURE 25

A Simple Input-Output Total
Requirements Table

(Total Requirements Coefficients: Total
Requirements per Unit of Final Delivery)

Every Unit of Delivery to Final Demand by / Requires Total Sales by	Agriculture	Manufacturing
Agriculture	1.155+	0.868+
Manufacturing	0.072+	1.303+
Households	1.000	1.000
Total requirements from all sectors	2.227+	3.171+

The total requirements table provides total
sales by each sector per unit of output delivered
to final demand by any processing sector. In

Figure 25, for example, it can be seen that for every Mu. 1.00 of output delivered to final demand by agriculture, total sales by the agricultural sector to final demand, to itself, and to other processing sectors (in this case, there is only one other), will be slightly more than Mu. 1.155. And total sales by manufacturing to all processing sectors will be slightly more than Mu. 0.072. If primary sales are added in, total sales by all suppliers in the economy to all purchasers will be slightly more than Mu. 2.227 per Mu. 1.00 of output delivered to final demand by agriculture. Mu. 1.00 of the Mu. 2.227 total represents sales to final demand; Mu. 1.00 represents sales by primary suppliers, and Mu. 0.227 represents interindustry transactions. The manufacturing column of Figure 25 can be explained in a similar fashion.

Now, let us return once again to the final demand estimate for the island economy. Armed with the total requirements table, it would be unnecessary to compute total input requirements by the iterative method as was done in Figure 23. In effect, this has been done in advance through the computation of total requirements coefficients. All that need be done now is to multiply the coefficients in each column of the total requirements table by the corresponding final demand estimate.

Figure 26 shows these computations for the island economy example. The column for agriculture in Figure 26 shows total sales by each supplier required to satisfy the anticipated Mu. 200,000 of delivery to final demand by agriculture. The manufacturing column provides the same information for the anticipated Mu. 100,000 of delivery to final demand by manufacturing. The "total" column corresponds to the bottom row of Figure 23 and shows total sales by each supplier for the combined Mu. 300,000 of delivery to final demand.

The total for each column can easily be disaggregated into its final demand, primary supplies, and interindustry sales components. Of the

FIGURE 26

Illustrative Total Requirements Computations
from Total Requirements Table
(Thousands of Monetary Units)

Final Delivery by / Requires Total Sales by	Agriculture	Manufacturing	Total
Agriculture	200 x 1.155+ = 231+	100 x 0.868+ = 86.8+	317.8+
Manufacturing	200 x 0.072+ = 14.4+	100 x 1.303+ = 130.3+	144.7+
Households	200 x 1 = 200	100 x 1 = 100	300.0
Total	200 x 2.227+ = 445.4+	100 x 3.171+ = 317.1+	762.5+

approximate Mu. 762,500 of total output, for example, we know that Mu. 300,000 represents anticipated sales to final demand; Mu. 300,000 represents sales of primary suppliers (income, or value added); and the remainder, Mu. 162,500, represents total interindustry sales.

All the foregoing, based on a highly simplified numerical example, comprises but a superficial introduction to input-output concepts and the input-output tables. The following sections of this chapter will consider input-output analysis in light of some of the real-world considerations that

confront the regional analyst. While what follows
is also a relatively superficial treatment of the
subject, it will be meaningful and useful only to
the reader with a thorough understanding of what
has gone before.

THE TRANSACTIONS TABLE

Figure 27 provides a sample format for a regional input-output transactions table. It is considerably more complex than the transactions table
of Figure 21, for the highly simplified island
economy.

As a matter of convenience, input and output
summaries have been added to the transactions table
to provide a framework for recapitulation. Inside
the double lines, the data matrix can be divided
into four quadrants. The upper right is the final
demand quadrant; this shows sales of commodities
produced in the region by each regional processing
supplier to each major, final demand sector. The
upper left is the interindustry quadrant, the heart
of the input-output accounts and shows interindustry sales by regional processing suppliers listed
at the left to regional processing purchasers listed at the top. The lower left is the final payments or primary inputs quadrant and shows sales by
primary suppliers to regional processing sectors.
The lower right is the final payments-final demand
quadrant, which records sales by primary suppliers
to final purchasers (some of the sales of imports
sectors to exports sectors indicated in this quadrant will have zero values because regional agents
are not involved). The data for the transactions
table represent total sales that have involved any
element of the regional economy during the study
year.

In the transactions table, as in subsequent
tables, the regional processing sectors are listed
from left to right along the top, and from top to
bottom along the left side. In Figure 27,

FIGURE 27

Expanded Transactions Table Format

| | | | Purchasing Sectors | | | | | | Final Demand | | | | | | | Output Summary | | |
| | | | Regional Processing Sectors | | | | | | Local | | | Export | | | Net inventory change | | | |
			Industry 1	Industry 2	· · ·	Industry i	· · ·	Industry n	Households	Investment	Government	Households	Business	Central government		Total regional processing sectors	Total final demand	Total output
Supplying Sectors	Regional Processing Sectors	Industry 1	x_{11}	x_{12}	· · ·	x_{1i}	· · ·	x_{1n}										
		Industry 2	x_{21}	x_{22}	· · ·	x_{2i}	· · ·	x_{2n}										
		· · ·	·	·	· · · ·	·	· · · ·	·										
		Industry i	x_{i1}	x_{i2}	· · ·	x_{ii}	· · ·	x_{in}										
		· · ·	·	·	· · · ·	·	· · · ·	·										
		Industry n	x_{n1}	x_{n2}	· · ·	x_{ni}	· · ·	x_{nn}										
	Final Payments	Local Households																
		Gross business savings																
		Government																
		Imports Labor																
		Transfers to parent companies																
		Central government																
		Processed goods																
		Others																
Input Summary		Total regionally processed inputs																
		Total final payments																
		Total outlay																

144

unconventional notation has been employed in using
the subscripts "i" and "n" for both columns and
rows. This has been done in order to emphasize the
fact that precisely the same list of industries
that process products in the region appears at the
top and left of the interindustry quadrant.

For purposes of regional analysis, processing
suppliers and purchasers are those that are located
in the region. Imported supplies, whether processed or not, are not processed inputs from the
point of view of the regional economy because they
do not require locally produced inputs for their
production. Similarly, export sales, whether for
intermediate or final uses, are not intermediate
sales from the standpoint of the regional economy
because they are not used for further processing
within the region.

Unless the sources supplying the necessary
sales data maintain exceptionally good records and
are uniquely cooperative, the input-output analyst
is likely to find that, for many industries, total
purchases (inputs, or outlays) will not equal total
sales (output, or product). It is common practice
in such cases to add an additional row and column,
both entitled <u>undistributed</u>. These are "dummies"
in which residual discrepancies between the input
and output totals are indicated and thus bring them
into equality. More than accounting hocus-pocus,
the undistributed row and column account for actual
purchases or sales that the analyst is unable to
distribute among the sectors because of data im-
perfections.

In input-output accounting, as in other forms
of accounting, it is customary to attribute to the
<u>trade sector</u> (wholesale and retail trade) only the
value of sales that represents <u>gross margin</u> (sales
less cost of goods sold). If the goods sold by the
trade sector were treated as inputs, other regional
processing industries would show few, if any, sales
to final demand. The bulk of sales to final demand
would be registered in the trade sector because the

larger part of the final sales of most industries
reach consumers and, indeed, many intermediate users as well, through wholesalers and retailers.
Hence, sales of suppliers are recorded in accordance with the purchaser for which they are destined,
whether or not the trade sector intervenes. This
practice does not alter the value of total output,
and it may be violated in cases where it is important to trace flows precisely and to highlight
trade-sector linkages.

Final demand (final sales, or final uses) includes all output destinations other than regional
processing sectors; therefore, it has both local
and foreign components. Locally, in addition to
households, sales for investment and sales to government represent final sales, and there may be
others. Investment includes replacement as well as
growth investment. Since it is not net of depreciation, it is often called gross investment or
gross capital formation. Even though investment
sales may be to regional processing sectors, they
are not considered intermediate because the goods
purchases receive no further processing and are not
resold. Export sales, in addition to household,
include those to businesses (whether for investment
or intermediate uses), those to the central government, and possibly others. Net inventory change
also represents a final use with respect to the regional economy for the accounting year.

In Figure 27, the term "final payments" has
been substituted for "primary inputs," used previously. This has been done in order to emphasize
that payments received by these suppliers do not
result in further payments to regional processing
sectors for inputs.

Customarily, wages, salaries, profits, property income, and other sources of personal income are
consodiered final payments to households. In some
cases, it may be desirable to disaggregate these
by type of payment. In addition to households,
local final payments include gross business savings

(including capital consumption allowances that either were made or ought to have been made to cover depreciation) and payments to government. All payments for goods and services imported to the region are considered final payments in the regional transactions table. Figure 27 provides examples of categories of imports that might be itemized.

The final demand columns and final payments rows contain information that corresponds to the income and product accounts. Indeed, with some slight statistical adjustments, they can and often do serve as a crosscheck for independent regional income and product accounting.

Total output and total outlay (input) should be equal for each of the regional processing sectors. As presented in Figure 27, these totals cannot vary from total outlays for inputs. Any deviation of total sales (including undistributed sales) from total outlays should be accounted for by a positive or negative net inventory change. An alternative to this approach is to replace the net inventory change column with an inventory additions column and an inventory depletions row.

The illustrative transactions table format shown in Figure 27 is relatively detailed. In fact, it is more so than may be necessary or feasible in the case of most underdeveloped regions. If only the interindustry quadrant is of real concern to the analyst, the final demand and final payments categories may be combined into a single column and row, respectively.

The definition of industries, level of disaggregation, determination of exogenous and endogenous sectors, and the like must remain matters for careful consideration in each individual case. Decisions regarding these matters will reflect unique regional characteristics; the analytical orientation of the input-output study; data availability; assumptions; and perhaps even social, cultural, and political factors. There are only two ironclad

rules. First, the list of regional processing purchasers must be identical with the list of regional
processing suppliers. And second, accounting procedures must distinguish in a meaningful way between regional processing sectors and final demand
categories on the one hand, and between regional
processing sectors and final payments categories on
the other.

THE DIRECT REQUIREMENTS TABLE

As can be seen in Figure 28, the full direct
requirements table format is essentially the same
as that used in the island economy example. As before, direct requirements coefficients are computed
by dividing through each regional processing column
of the transactions table by the column total. Final demand columns do not appear because, by definition, their purchases are not for intermediate
use (and therefore not truly inputs), from the region's standpoint.

Frequently, final payments categories are combined into a single, primary inputs row in the direct requirements table, as has been done in Figure
28. However, in many cases, it will be desirable
to retain primary inputs disaggregation in order to
observe the distribution among the various categories of final payments "leakages" from the streams
of interindustry purchases.

Each data cell in the direct requirements table
contains a technical coefficient that indicates the
input required by the industry at the top from the
industry at the left for each unit of output delivered by the industry at the top. Since each column
must total to one, there can appear no values in
excess of one. For any estimated or hypothesized
output of any regional processing industry, direct
input requirements from all suppliers can be computed by multiplying each of the coefficients in
the appropriate column by the total output figure.

FIGURE 28

Expanded Direct Requirements Table Format

		Purchasing Sectors					
		Industry 1	Industry 2	· · ·	Industry i	· · ·	Industry n
Supplying Sectors	Industry 1	X_{11}	X_{12}	· · ·	X_{1i}	· · ·	X_{1n}
	Industry 2	X_{21}	X_{22}	· · ·	X_{2i}	· · ·	X_{2n}
	· · ·	· · ·	· · ·	· · · ·	· · ·	· · · ·	· · ·
	Industry i	X_{i1}	X_{i2}	· · ·	X_{ii}	· · ·	X_{in}
	· · ·	· · ·	· · ·	· · · ·	· · ·	· · · ·	· · ·
	Industry n	X_{n1}	X_{n2}	· · ·	X_{ni}	· · ·	X_{nn}
	Total regionally produced inputs						
	Total primary inputs						
Total direct inputs		1.00	1.00	· · ·	1.00	· · ·	1.00

THE TOTAL REQUIREMENTS TABLE

The conventional total requirements table format is essentially the same as the direct requirements table format. In the case of the total requirements table, each cell in the data matrix
shows total sales by the industry at the left when
the industry at the top delivers one unit of output
to final demand.

It is important to note that the coefficient
which appears in any cell does not indicate which
industries purchased the input supplied by the industry at the left. The total requirements coefficients includes indirect inputs sold to all intermediate purchasers as well as direct inputs sold to
the industry at the top of the column.

In the total requirements table, all the cells
of the major diagonal of the data matrix, where
each regional processing industry's row and column
intersect, will have values greater than one (in
some cases equal to one, but never less than one).
This is because these coefficients reflect not only
direct and indirect requirements but also the one
unit of delivery to final demand. All other coefficients in any column will be smaller than the coefficient in the major diagonal. Apart from its
conceptual significance, this characteristic of the
total requirements table can serve as an aid in
spotting computational error.

In order to use the total requirements table
as a simulation-projection device, estimates of
final demand must be supplied from elsewhere. All
the coefficients in each column are multiplied by
the given final demand estimate for the industry at
the top. Column totals will then show total outputs required from all regional processing industries in combination in order to enable satisfac-
tion of the given final demand by the industry at
the top. Row totals will show total output required from the regional processing industry at the
left in order for the regional economy as a whole

to satisfy the entire set of the individual industry's final demand estimates.

We should now reconsider the method for solving the direct requirements table for the total requirements coefficients. Earlier, the iterative
method was demonstrated with a set of hypothetical
final demand estimates. Then it was pointed out
that if this procedure were followed on an industry-
by-industry basis for a single unit of delivery to
final demand by each industry, it would provide the
total requirements coefficient.

It was also noted that an indication of nearness to limit values of the iterative process is
given by the nearness of total primary inputs to
final demand. In other words, this is the nearness
to one when solving for total requirements coefficients. But what is to be done once it has been
determined by this means (or some other basis) that
the iterative method has been worked out "far
enough"? In the earlier examples, the iterations
were simply stopped at this point, and the figures
for each sector were summed for total requirements.
This is not an entirely satisfactory procedure,
however, and it leaves the analyst with the uncom-
fortable feeling that one more round would bring
him one degree closer to "actual" values.

Fortunately, a procedure exists for rounding
off, that is, estimating for each sector the total
value encompassed by all the rounds that remain uncomputed after the cutoff point. There are five
steps in the procedure, as follows:

Step 1. For each sector, compute the ratio of
the increment in the last round to the increment in
the next to the last round.

Step 2. Compute the average of these ratios
among all the sectors.

Step 3. Compute the ratio of this average to
one minus this average.

Step 4. For each sector, multiply the increment in the last round by the ratio from step 3. This gives the approximation of the sum of the remaining uncomputed increments for each sector.

Step 5. Add these quantities to the totals for the respective sectors.

Empirical tests have shown that this procedure provides an extremely close approximation to the actual limit of the iterative process.

Application of the rounding-off procedure can be demonstrated by reference to the island economy example used earlier. It was mentioned that the total requirements table for the island economy was developed by the iterative method that went through six rounds and was truncated. Following are the results of the iteration computations for one unit of delivery to final demand by agriculture:

	Agriculture	Manufacturing
Final demand	1.00	
Direct requirements	0.10	0.05
Indirect requirements		
Round 1	0.0400000	0.015000
Round 2	0.0094000	0.005000
Round 3	0.0039400	0.001470
Round 4	0.0012760	0.000491
Round 5	0.0004222	0.000162
Total (final demand + 6 rounds)	1.1550382	0.072123

Now, instead of truncating, the rounding-off procedure can be applied.

Step 1. Agriculture: $\dfrac{0.0004222}{0.0012760}$ = 0.331

Manufacturing: $\dfrac{0.000162}{0.000491}$ = 0.330

Step 2. $\dfrac{0.331 + 0.330}{2}$ = 0.3305

Step 3. $\dfrac{0.3305}{1 - 0.3305}$ = $\dfrac{0.3305}{0.6695}$ = 0.494

Step 4. Agriculture   (0.494) (0.0004222)
$$= 0.0002085668$$

Manufacturing (0.494) (0.0001620)
$$= 0.0000800280$$

Step 5. Agriculture   1.1550382 + 0.0002085668
$$= 1.155247$$

Manufacturing 0.0721230 + 0.0000800280
$$= 0.072203$$

When we repeat the entire procedure for one unit of
delivery to final demand by manufacturing, the following results:

Agriculture: 0.869551

Manufacturing: 1.304351

To summarize, we take the iterative method to six
rounds and then apply the rounding-off procedure
which produces the following total requirements coefficients for the island economy. One unit of delivery to final demand by: <u>Agriculture Manufacturing</u>

Results in total sales as
follows:

	Agriculture	Manufacturing
Agriculture	1.1552	0.8696
Manufacturing	0.0722	1.3044

While the rounding-off procedure enables greater precision, it also adds to the cumbersomeness of the iterative method. Clearly, when one works by hand or even with a desk calculator, the number of sectors that can be handled within reasonable limits of time and manpower, using the iterative method, is limited. At some point (usually when the interindustry matrix covers about fifteen to twenty regional processing sectors), the time and cost involved in ensuring errorfree computations makes it worthwhile to employ computers to do the job, even if these are unavailable locally. The iterative method involves no unusual programing, and any computer center anywhere in the world, if supplied with the direct requirements table and written instructions concerning how it is to be processed, should be able to supply printouts covering any number of iterations, plus the rounding-off procedure, quickly and at minimum cost.

However, when absolute accuracy is more important than individual, round computations, as is usually the case, there is an alternative method for solving for the total requirements coefficient. This method, which is used nearly universally, is known as the matrix inverse method. Unless the interindustry matrix covers but a handful of regional processing sectors, the matrix inverse method can be accomplished only by computer. The method involves performing a series of mechanical, mathematical operations on the direct requirements table and thereby converts it to the total requirements table. The coefficients that appear in the total requirements table computed by the matrix inverse method represent the actual limits of the iterative process, limits that can never be fully attained through the iterative method. In fact, in much of the input-output literature, the total requirements table is referred to as the "matrix inverse table."

It is not necessary for the analyst to know the operations involved in the matrix inverse method. It is a standard mathematical procedure, and most computers will be able to use built-in or

"canned" programs (which, incidentally, substantially reduces the cost involved). All the analyst
need do is supply the matrix of direct requirements
coefficients and request a $(I - A)^{-1}$ solution. In
linear algebraic notation, this means the inverse
of the matrix formed by subtracting the A matrix
from the identity matrix. In this case, A is the
matrix of the direct requirements coefficient.

For the interested reader, there follows a
brief description of the six steps involved in computing the total requirements table by the matrix
inverse method. The presentation assumes a background in basic linear algebra, and it uses the
interindustry matrix of the direct requirements
table from the island economy example, Figure 22,
as the A matrix. The end result is Figure 29, the
total requirements table for the island economy.
Even readers not concerned with the operations involved in the matrix inverse method will be interested in comparing Figure 29 with the total requirements table computed by the iterative method,
Figure 25, and to the coefficients produced by the
rounding-off procedure discussed above.

Step 1. Write the direct requirement coefficients for regional processing sectors in matrix
form.

$$\begin{bmatrix} 0.10 & 0.60 \\ 0.05 & 0.20 \end{bmatrix}$$

Step 2. Subtract this matrix from the identity matrix, and give the (I - A) matrix.

$$\begin{bmatrix} 0.90 & -0.60 \\ -0.05 & 0.80 \end{bmatrix}$$

Step 3. Compute the determinant of the (I - A) matrix.

$$(0.90) \ (0.80) - (-0.60) \ (-0.05)$$

$$= \qquad 0.72 - 0.03 = 0.69$$

Step 4. Cofactor the (I - A) matrix.

$$\begin{bmatrix} 0.80 & 0.05 \\ 0.60 & 0.90 \end{bmatrix}$$

Step 5. Transpose the cofactored matrix, and give the matrix adjoint.

$$\begin{bmatrix} 0.80 & 0.60 \\ 0.05 & 0.90 \end{bmatrix}$$

Step 6. Divide the adjoint by the determinant of the (I - A) matrix, computed in Step 3, and give $(I - A)^{-1}$.

$$\begin{bmatrix} 1.1594 & 0.8706 \\ 0.0725 & 1.3043 \end{bmatrix}$$

The total requirements table developed through the matrix inverse method will be completely accurate except, of course, for inaccuracies that result from rounding. The reader may find it an enlightening exercise to apply the final demand figures from the island economy example to the total requirements table in Figure 29. The final demand estimates were Mu. 200,000 for agriculture and Mu. 100,000 for manufacturing. The results should be compared with those obtained in Figure 26, in which

FIGURE 29

Total Requirements Coefficients,
Matrix Inverse Method

		Every Unit of Delivery to Final Demand by	
		Agriculture	Manufacturing
Requires Total Sales by	Agriculture	1.1594	0.8706
	Manufacturing	0.0725	1.3043
	Total regionally produced inputs	1.2319	2.1749
	Total primary inputs	1.0000	1.0000
Total requirements, all sectors		2.2319	3.1749

the final demand estimates were applied to the total requirements coefficients derived through the
iterative method.

If disaggregation of primary inputs has been
retained in the direct requirements table, this
disaggregation can be retained when employing the
iterative method, so that the total requirements
table also shows primary input detail. The matrix
inverse method, however, handles only the square
data matrix of the regional processing sectors.
Thus, when the matrix inverse method is used, if
primary inputs are to be represented by more than a
single row, the detail has to be "built back in"
after the total requirements coefficients for the
regional processing sectors have been computed.

In order to demonstrate how this can be done,
we shall turn to the island economy example for the
last time. The interindustry matrix of the total
requirements table has been derived by the matrix
inverse method, and it appears in Figure 29. However, the direct requirements table of Figure 30
will replace that of Figure 22. The only difference between the two is that in Figure 30 there are
two primary inputs categories, households and government.

FIGURE 30

Illustrative Direct Requirements Table with
Disaggregated Primary Inputs

Purchasing Sectors / Supplying Sectors		Agriculture	Manufacturing
Regionally processed inputs	Agriculture	0.10	0.60
	Manufacturing	0.05	0.20
Primary inputs	Households	0.60	0.15
	Government	0.25	0.05
Total direct inputs		1.00	1.00

We know that if households and government were
combined into a single, primary inputs row in the
total requirements table, the total requirements

coefficient appearing in every cell of that row
would be one. It has been decided by the analyst,
however, that households and government should each
be represented by a row in the total requirements
table so that their total requirements coefficients
can be considered separately.

Each of these coefficients can be computed as
the sum of the products resulting from the multiplication of the corresponding direct requirements
table row by the total requirements table interindustry column. Consider, for example, the total
requirements coefficient for households in the agriculture column of the total requirements table.
This would be the sum of products that resulted
from the multiplication of the coefficients in the
household row of the direct requirements table
(Figure 30), by the corresponding coefficients in
the agriculture column of the total requirements
table (Figure 29).

The computations for the four primary inputs
total requirements coefficients in the example are
provided in Figure 31. Figure 32 shows how the results of these computations would appear in the total requirements table with disaggregated primary
inputs.

The reader with a background in linear algebra
will recognize the procedure described as nothing
more than a matrix multiplication. This operation
can also be handled by the computer, for very little, if any, extra cost. If disaggregated primary
inputs total requirements coefficients are desired,
the correct instruction to the computer operators
would be: Multiply the matrix of primary inputs
direct requirements coefficients (the premultiplier)
by the $(I - A)^{-1}$ matrix (postmultiplier), and append
the product matrix to the bottom of the $I - A^{-1}$
matrix. The computer printout will show the complete matrix of regional processing and primary
inputs total requirements coefficients. All that
will remain to be done is to write in the names of
the sectors at the left and top and, of course, it
can be arranged for the computer to do this as well.

FIGURE 31

Computation of Total Requirements Coefficients for Primary Inputs

Primary Inputs Are Required by	When Delivery to Final Demand Is Made by					
	Agriculture			Manufacturing		
	Agr.	Mfg.	Total	Agr.	Mfg.	Total
And Are Supplied by						
Households	0.6 x 1.1594 = 0.6956	0.15 x 0.0725 = 0.0109	0.7065	0.6 x 0.8706 = 0.5224	0.15 x 1.3043 = 0.1956	0.718
Government	0.25 x 1.1594 = 0.2899	0.05 x 0.0725 = 0.0036	0.2935	0.25 x 0.8706 = 0.2176	0.05 x 1.3043 = 0.0652	0.2828

FIGURE 32

Illustrative Total Requirements Table with
Disaggregated Primary Inputs

Every Unit of Delivery to Final Demand by Requires Total Sales by		Agriculture	Manufacturing
Regionally processed inputs	Agriculture	1.1594	0.8706
	Manufacturing	0.0725	1.3043
Primary inputs	Households	0.7065	0.7180
	Government	0.2935	0.2828

INTERREGIONAL INPUT-OUTPUT STUDIES

Imagine a region that exports coal and simple
metal products. One of its principal customers for
coal is the country's single steel mill, located
elsewhere. National projections show a rapidly increasing demand for metal products. An input-
output model has been constructed for the region,
and it shows that in order to satisfy the greater
demand for its metal products, the region will require, among other things, substantially increased
imports of steel inputs. However, the input-output
tables do not show that as a consequence of the region's increased demand for steel imports, it will
have to supply greater quantities of coal exports
to the steel mill.

Or imagine a region with several small craft
industries. The products of these industries, as

well as many agricultural products, are marketed
through a trading center outside the region. Projections show a growing regional population, and
the regional input-output model indicates increased
imports to satisfy the growth in final demand by
local households. What the input-output tables do
not show is that the increase in imports, purchased
in large part directly or indirectly through the
trading center outside the region, will result in a
substantial increase in exports, because many of
the imported goods originate in the region.

Interregional feedback effects like these can
be introduced into the input-output analysis through
an interregional input-output framework. In this
framework, the list of processing sectors is repeated at the top of the table to the right of the
list for the study region, and at the left of the
table below the list for the study region, for each
additional region covered by the interregional
input-output study. For this purpose, the rest of
the country may be considered the single "other"
region, or any number of subnational regions may be
included. Thus, for any processed input that is
imported to the study region, the transactions table will indicate the region and industry from
which it was imported. Similarly, the destination
region and industry for exports of the study region
will be indicated. If only interregional transactions with the study region are to be considered,
the table will be "doglegged," that is, there will
be no data matrixes that represent transactions between the other regions exclusively.

An interregional input-output study is a major
undertaking, and, unfortunately, it is usually beyond the capabilities and resources of a regional
development staff. In any event, such a study can
be performed most effectively at the national level.
A meaningful description of the procedures involved,
therefore, is beyond the scope of this book. Isard
(1960), in Chapter 8, provides a good introduction
to interregional input-output studies, and the subject is covered in other publications listed in the
References and in the Bibliography.

In the absence of a full-fledged interregional input-output study, information on interregional linkages and feedback effects must be derived from a source beyond the framework of regional input-output analysis. Data from <u>linkages, flows</u>, and similar studies with an interregional orientation can provide the basis for final demand estimates that will reflect the impact of interregional interdependence.

CONSIDERATIONS IN PERFORMING AND USING A REGIONAL INPUT-OUTPUT STUDY

Many of the operational considerations in performing a regional input-output study have been covered in various contexts, earlier, There remain, however, a number of major, unresolved problems that the analyst will confront and have to deal with as appropriate in each individual case. Understandably, these problems increase with the complexity of the economy being studied, but then, so does the usefulness of input-output analysis.

The most obvious difficulty in using input-output tables as a simulation model is the problem of <u>constant coefficients</u>. In fact, technical production coefficients are a function of the mix of specific products being produced, supply and market prices, the technology of production processes, the technology of materials inputs, external economies, input delivery times and reliabilities, binding contracts, traditional trade patterns, and more. Empirical studies have shown, however, that despite changing technologies, prices, and other factors, technical coefficients of major aggregates change relatively slowly. The greater the industry detail in the tables and rate of innovation in the region, the less reliable will be the technical coefficients developed in the study for long-run simulation purposes.

An approach to estimating changes in technical coefficients that is based on studies of technologically "leading" industries has been tried, as have

other methods for dealing with the problem of constant coefficients. None of the attempted solutions has met with widespread, overt enthusiasm on
the part of regional workers. However, in some
cases, these methods may provide more rational ways
of dealing with the problem than ignoring it alto-
gether. A particularly interesting and instructive
attempt to deal with the problem of constant coefficients is described by Miernyk et al. (1970).

     The fact that final payments are not always
final and final demand is not always exogenous may
also create a problem for the analyst. The most
obvious example is labor. An increase in the demand for labor will result in increased incomes to
households, which may, in turn, increase final demand, and therefore interindustry sales, even in
the current period. Other examples were given in
the above discussion on interregional input-output
studies.

     Several problems in input-output accounting
are related to time concepts. Actual transactions
during a single accounting year constitute the basis for the entire input-output structure. Any
particular year may involve "irregularities" that
bring the reliability of the coefficients derived
from the transactions data into question. Such irregularities may include major strikes, passing
fads, unusually large inventories, and other tem-
porary influences on the regional economy.

     Then there is the problem that stems from the
fact that input purchases during one accounting
year reflect not only current output, but, to some
extent, anticipated output in the next accounting
year, as well as inventory depletion that results
from sales in the previous accounting year. In
other words, in reality, the production process
does not follow the chronological pattern of the
input-output model precisely. Input purchases,
generally, are not made entirely in direct consequence of final demand in the current period, although, for all intents and purposes, they may do

so to a significant degree. This problem is reduced if "inputs" are counted to reflect consumption in the process of production rather than purchases by producers, an approach which, in turn,
introduces new and often complex problems of data
collection and reliability.

The regional input-output analyst is, of
course, plagued with the usual probems of disclosure, data reliability, and the cost of data collection. Data problems are particularly acute in
input-output analysis because of the level of detail that is required and the <u>compounding of error</u>
in the process of derivation of the total requirements table.

To all this may be added the problem of prices.
Actual sales data may be found to be incomplete or
unavailable. In such cases, estimation will require the "pricing" of physical output. This may
be quite difficult because most goods sell at one
price for consumers and at another for producers
who use them as intermediate products. Which set
of prices should the analyst use? Furthermore,
there is usually a gap between quoted and actual
prices, in consequence of special agreements, bulk
purchasing, and so on. Then, prices change during
the year in accordance with seasonal variations or
as the result of inflationary pressures. The problem of pricing is a rather important one, not only
because transactions data provide the basis for the
drivation of technical coefficients, but also because they may provide the basis for conversion of
findings of the input-output study into labor terms.

Many of these problems can be overcome by
careful backup research and by analytical ingenuity.
Some, however, are inherent in the input-output approach and cannot be divorced from it. This approach involves the <u>basic assumption</u> that <u>each industry can be represented by a single, linear,
homogeneous production function</u>. Therefore, first,
each industry produces only <u>one product</u> (conceptually), and <u>produces it uniquely</u> and by a <u>single</u>

production process. Second, input purchases by an
industry are related only to--and change in direct
proportion to--the level of current output of that
industry. And third, there are no external economies or diseconomies, and, therefore, the effect of
simultaneous production by several different industries is equal to the sum of their separate effects.
The basic assumption requires various degrees of
departure from reality, and the degree depends on
the specific case.

Despite its apparent shortcomings, there is a
trend toward the increased use of the input-output
model in regional analysis. It has been found to
be a powerful and instructive tool and yields many
insights otherwise unavailable. Also, perhaps sur-
prisingly, it is an extremely flexible tool, adjust-
able to specific needs of many kinds, and compati-
ble with and complementary to many other analysis
methods, such as mix-and-share and economic base
analysis.

In many cases, the chief value of input-output
analysis may be its descriptive rather than its
predictive capabilities, and these can be exploited
to a significant degree even if the total requirements table is not computed. As a descriptive
tool, input-output tables present an enormous quantity of information in a concise and orderly fashion, provide a comprehensive interindustry picture,
and point up the strategic importance of various
sectors. Input-output analysis may therefore highlight the true sources of regional growth in a way
not possible with any other method of analysis.

The process of compiling the transactions
table, the major task in performing an input-output
study, may itself yield unexpected benefits. This
activity provides the development staff with the
opportunity to trace through the economic structure
of the region in a systematic fashion. It also re-
veals data gaps and provides the opportunity for
finding ways of overcoming them. And the data collected for the transactions table are useful for

many other kinds of studies, regional accounts being the most obvious among them.

The use of the input-output model as a projection device requires independent final demand estimates. Hence, the reliability of the projections it produces will be at least as speculative as the final demand estimates that are applied to it. Nevertheless, guessing the future is often an important part of the planning process, and the input-output model may provide the best available means of guessing.

Input-output analysis has perhaps been used most widely for selective simulation. This includes, among others, first, simulating the impacts of alternative levels of final demand in specific sectors; and second, simulating the impacts of changes in the regional economic structure that express themselves as altered technical coefficients.

Suppose it has been decided to expand a certain sector of the regional economy. The regional development planner must consider the adjustments necessary in order to accommodate this expansion and derive maximum benefit to the region from it. For example, what other sectors will have to be expanded, and by how much? What other sectors will gain through increased inputs availability? What kinds of preparatory training will be needed in the various sectors? What will be the full fiscal impact of the expansion? How will total employment, income, and demand be effected? What will be the full cost of the expansion to the region? Input-output analysis would either provide whole or partial answers to the planning questions posed or essential information inputs needed to develop the answers. For any one industry, a special-purpose study could be performed instead, and at less cost than input-output analysis. But an input-output study will provide a reusable tool for testing a limitless number of such situations, and with several side benefits in the bargain.

SUPPLEMENTARY ANALYTICAL TOOLS

Once the input-output transactions table is compiled, its immediate analytical value can be enhanced by reorganizing it into triangulated format. Triangulation involves listing the regional processing sectors by order of increasing structural interdependence.

The measure of structural interdependence, for purposes of triangulation, is the number of other sectors to which each sells its output. A perfectly triangulated interindustry quadrant of the transactions table would appear similar to that in Figure 33, in which each X represents interindustry sales, and a blank represents a zero value. Triangulation will never produce the perfectly symmetrical pattern shown in Figure 33 because of the relationships between an industry's inputs and its outputs; it should, however, produce a pattern that tends toward that direction. The triangulated order of industries, listed from top to bottom in accordance with increasing structural interdependence, should conform approximately to the order of industries when ranked in accordance with final sales as a decreasing proportion of total sales.

Triangulation provides immediate insights into the role of each industry in the regional network and into the hierarchical nature of the regional interindustry structure. These insights are of major analytical value and carry over into subsequent phases of the input-output study.

Many input-output analysts have found it helpful to assemble a destination of output table. For each industry, including primary suppliers, the percent of total output sold to processing sectors as a group and to final demand sectors as a group is computed, on the basis of data in the transactions table. Industries are then listed in the destination of output table in rank order by ascending or descending percentages of the total output sold to regional processing sectors. The percentage

FIGURE 33

Triangulated Interindustry Quadrant, Transactions Table

	Retail trade	Construction	Hotels and tourism	Personal services	Fisheries	Quarries	Agriculture	Wholesale trade	Food products	Real estate	Crafts	Utilities and transport	Final Demand
Regional Processing Sectors	Regional Processing Sectors												Final Demand
Retail trade	X												
Construction	X	X											
Hotels and tourism	X	X	X										
Personal services	X	X	X	X									
Fisheries	X	X	X	X	X								
Quarries	X	X	X	X	X	X							
Agriculture	X	X	X	X	X	X	X						
Wholesale trade	X	X	X	X	X	X	X	X					
Food products	X	X	X	X	X	X	X	X	X				
Real estate	X	X	X	X	X	X	X	X	X	X			
Crafts	X	X	X	X	X	X	X	X	X	X	X		
Utilities and transport	X	X	X	X	X	X	X	X	X	X	X	X	

Purchased by / Supplied by

Regional Processing Sectors

Final Payments

of output destined for each of the two categories
of users, intermediate and final, is also shown.

From the input-output direct requirements table, a sources of inputs table can be assembled.
For each regional processing column, coefficients
that represent regionally processed inputs are
summed. Industries are then listed in the sources
of inputs table in rank order by ascending or descending percent of the total inputs from regional
processing suppliers. For each industry, the percent supplied by local processing sectors is shown,
and the number of supplying sectors is indicated.

There are numerous additional types of relatively simple supplementary devices that can help
highlight the analytical significance of the findings of an input-output study and thereby enhance
its descriptive value. Additional suggestions
along these lines will be found among the works
listed in this chapter's References. The article
by Leontief (1963), represents a good starting
point.

SHORTCUTS

The major task in assembling an input-output
model is the collection of the relatively large
quantity of transactions data. Because capabilities
for accomplishing this are often limited, and this
is especially so in underdeveloped regions, attempts have been made by several students of input-
output analysis to develop shortcuts that will reduce the magnitude of the data collection task.

One frequently used shortcut is known as the
rows only method. It is often possible to obtain
data for total shipments or sales of a sector but
not for individual establishments. If this is the
case, the analyst might attempt to distribute total
sales among the purchasing sectors on the basis of
information obtained from a selected sample of establishments in the supplying sector. The surveyed

establishments need only be asked to provide information on the percentage distribution of shipments
or sales among purchasing sectors. Firms will generally be more cooperative in supplying information
when money values are not requested.

Following this procedure on a sector-by-sector
basis provides the distribution among purchasers of
the output for each row. Of course, when all the
rows are filled in, the columns will also be filled
in. The disadvantages in this shortcut method are
that the distribution of sales is based on an indirect estimating procedure, and the benefit of a
crosscheck by an independent determination of input
data is lost.

The Technique for Area Planning (TAP method),
discussed in the publication by the Regional Economic Development Institute (1967), provides an
alternative shortcut of a completely different nature. In order to be suitable for application of
the TAP method, the region must have the following
characteristics: First, it must feature a relatively small number of leading sectors (preferably,
individual establishments) for which relatively
complete transactions data can be obtained. Second,
other sectors must each be relatively small and of
lesser importance in terms of over-all analysis.
Third, minimum aggregate regional data must be
available or capable of being estimated with reasonable accuracy. And fourth, the index of regional specialization must be at least 0.20 and preferably 0.25.

The index of regional specialization is calculated in the following manner:

Step 1. Compute national and regional percentage distributions of employment, output, value
added, or revenues, by sector.

Step 2. For each sector, subtract the national from the regional percentage.

Step 3. Add up either the negative or the
positive differences (the total of negative differences will be equal to the total of positive differences).

Step 4. Divide the result by 100, in order to
express it as a decimal fraction.

Implementation of the TAP method requires
listing the regional processing sectors so that the
leading or major sectors are to the left and top,
and minor sectors are to the right and bottom along
the interindustry quadrant, as shown in Figure 34.
The cells containing an X in the data matrix of
Figure 34 are those that represent transactions between a major and some other sector and are the
only cells in the interindustry matrix for which
complete data are collected.

The remaining cells represent transactions between minor sectors and minor sectors. Each column
and row within this submatrix is handled as if it
were a single cell. In other words, a single sales
value is derived for each ⟨=====⟩, and it is not
distributed among the columns encompassed. Similarly, a single undistributed purchases total is
derived for each ⟨⟩ . Thus, time and expense are
reduced by ⟨⟩ minimizing detail where transactions among minor sectors exclusively are concerned.

Further detail concerning the TAP method, and
even a computer program for processing the data,
will be found in very readable form in the publication by the Regional Economic Development Institute.
Empirical tests have indicated that if applied under appropriate conditions, this technique will
generally produce results that deviate no more than
5 percent from results obtained through standard
input-output procedures performed at considerably
greater expense and effort.

In addition to the two shortcuts mentioned,
there are various sample survey techniques for

FIGURE 34

TAP Format, Interindustry Quadrant, Transactions Table

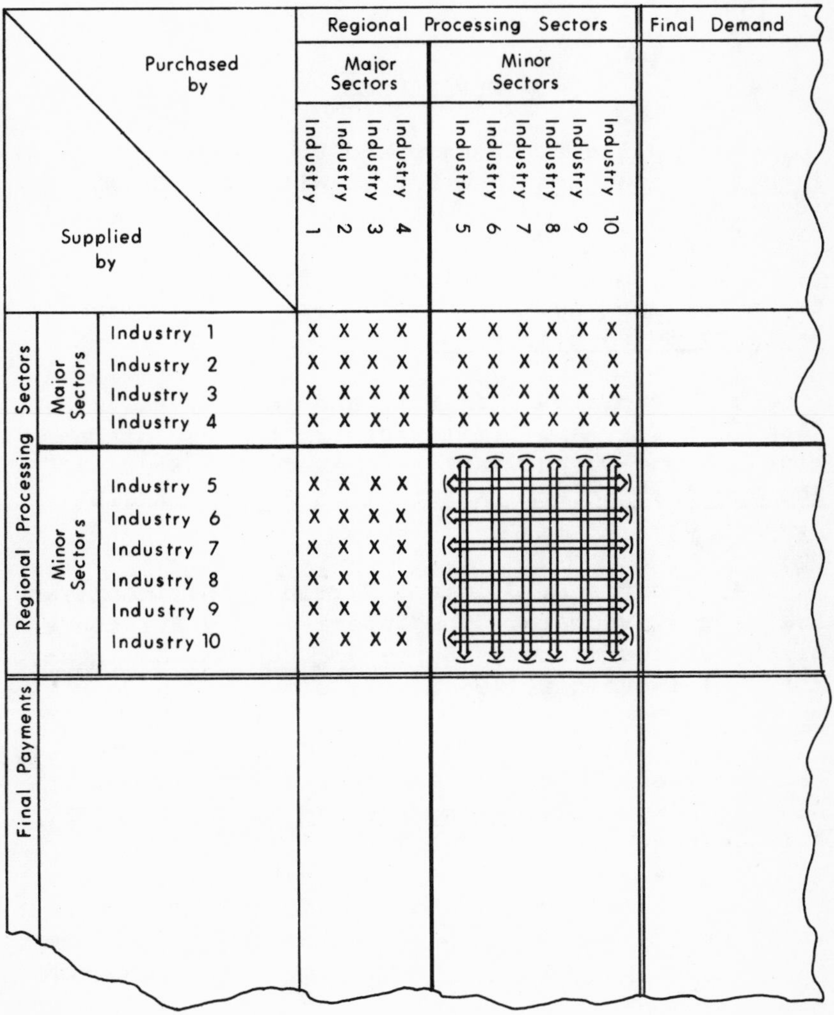
Regional Processing Sectors
Final Demand
Purchased by
Supplied by
Major Sectors
Minor Sectors
Industry 1
Industry 2
Industry 3
Industry 4
Industry 5
Industry 6
Industry 7
Industry 8
Industry 9
Industry 10
Regional Processing Sectors
Final Payments

reducing the cumbersome data collection problem.
These are mentioned among the literature listed in
the References and the Bibliography. Notable among
them is the discussion appearing in Miernyk (1970).
Some work has been done as well on nonsurvey techniques for estimating coefficients. For examples
of this, the reader is referred to Czamanski and
Malizia as well as Schaffer and Chu (both 1969), in
particular.

REFERENCES

1.   Hollis B. Chenery and Paul G. Clark, Interindustry Economics (New York: Wiley and Sons,
1959).

2.   John H. Cumberland, "A Regional Interindustry Model for Analysis of Development Objectives,"
Regional Science Association Papers, XVII (1966).

3.   Stanislaw Czamanski and Emil E. Malizia,
"Applicability and Limitations in the Use of National Input-Output Tables for Regional Studies,"
The Regional Science Association Papers, XXIII
(1969), 65-77.

4.   Morris R. Goldman, Martin L. Marimont, and
Beatrice N. Vaccara, "The Interindustry Structure
of the United States," Survey of Current Business,
XLIV, 11 (November, 1964), 10-30.

5.   William Lee Hansen and Charles M. Tiebout,
"An Intersectoral Flows Analysis of the California
Economy," Review of Economics and Statistics, XLV,
4 (November, 1963), 409-18.

6.   Walter Isard, "Interregional and Regional
Input-Output Analysis: A Model of a Space-Economy,"
Review of Economics and Statistics, XXXII (November,
1951), 318-28.

7.   Walter Isard, Methods of Regional Analysis:
An Introduction to Regional Science (New York: Massachusetts Institute of Technology and Wiley, 1960).

8.   Walter Isard, "Some Empirical Results and Problems of Regional Input-Output Analysis," Wasily W. Leontief, ed., Studies in the Structure of the American Economy (New York: Oxford University Press, 1953).

9.   Wassily W. Leontief, "Some Basic Problems of Empirical Input-Output Analysis," Input-Output Analysis: An Appraisal, Studies in Income and Wealth, Vol. XVIII, National Bureau of Economic Research (Princeton: Princeton University Press, 1955).

10.   Wassily W. Leontief, "The Structure of Development," Scientific American, CCIX, 23 (September, 1963), 148-66.

11.   William H. Miernyk, The Elements of Input-Output Analysis (New York: Random House, 1965).

12.   William H. Miernyk et al., Simulating Regional Economic Development (Lexington, Mass.: Heath Lexington Books, 1970).

13.   Leon N. Moses, "An Input-Output Linear Programming Approach to Interregional Analysis," Report, 1956-57 (Cambridge: Harvard Economic Research Project, 1957).

14.   Leon N. Moses, "The Stability of Interregional Trading Patterns and Input-Output Analysis," American Economic Review, XLV (December, 1955), 803-32.

15.   Regional Economic Development Institute, Incorporated, Technique for Area Planning (Washington, D.C.: U.S. Department of Commerce, Economic Development Administration, 1967).

16.   Roger Reifler and Charles M. Tiebout, "Interregional Input-Output: An Empirical California-Washington Model," Journal of Regional Science, X, 2 (August, 1970), 135-52.

17.   William A. Schaffer and Kong Chu, "Non-survey Techniques for Constructing Regional Inter-industry Models," The Regional Science Association Papers, XXIII (1969), 83-101.

18.   Charles M. Tiebout, The Community Economic Base Study, Supplementary Paper No. 16 (New York: Committee for Economic Development, 1962).

19.   Charles M. Tiebout, "Regional and Inter-regional Input-Output Models: An Appraisal," The Southern Economic Journal, XXIV, 2 (October, 1957), 140-47.

EXERCISES

1. Given the following data for Region Z in
19XX, complete an input-output analysis, including
a brief analytical interpretation and planning implications. Figures are in thousands of monetary
units.

	Total Sales	Sales to Regional Processing Sectors		
		Agriculture	Manufacturing	Services
Agricul-ture	2,500	500	1,130	100
Manufac-turing	1,500	20	120	40
Services	1,000	10	150	90

2. In the above example, what will be the impact if final demand for agricultural products
doubles?

3. What will happen to the interindustry
structure of the above example if technology in the
manufacturing sector changes such that double the
present proportion of inputs from itself are required at the expense of agriculture's proportion
of inputs to manufacturing?

BIBLIOGRAPHY

Books and Articles

1. Airov, Joseph. The Location of the Synthetic-fiber Industry: A Case Study in Regional Analysis. Cambridge: Massachusetts Institute of Technology and Wiley & Sons, 1959.

2. Alonso, William. Industrial Location and Regional Policy in Economic Development. Working Paper No. 74, Institute of Urban and Regional Development. Berkeley: University of California Press, 1968.

3. _____. Location and Land Use. Cambridge: Harvard University Press, 1964.

4. Andrews, Richard B. "Economic Planning for Small Areas: An Analytical System," Land Economics, XXXIX (May, 1963), 143-55.

5. _____. "Economic Planning for Small Areas: The Planning Process," Land Economics, XXXIX (August, 1963), 253-64.

6. Ashby, Lowell D. "The Geographic Redistribution of Employment: An Examination of the Elements of Change," Survey of Current Business, XLVI, 10 (October, 1964), 13-20.

7. Bachi, Roberto. "Standard Distance Measure and Related Methods for Spatial Analysis," Regional Science Association Papers and Proceedings, X (1963), 83-132.

8. Bachmura, Frank T., and Robert B. Glasgow, with discussion by M. H. Steinmueller. "Rural Area Development in a Growing Economy," Journal of Farm Economics, XLIII (December, 1961), 1532-40.

9. Barlowe, Raleigh. Land Resource Economics. Englewood Cliffs, N.J.: Prentice-Hall, 1958.

10. Barnum, H. G., R. Kasperson, and S. Kiuchi. Supplement through 1964 to Central Place Studies. Philadelphia: Regional Science Research Institute, 1965. (Also see Brian J. L. Berry and Allen Pred.)

11. Beckmann, Martin J. "City Hierarchies and the Distribution of City Size," Economic Development and Cultural Change, VI (1958), 243-48.

12. _____. "Some Reflections on Losch's Theory of Location," Papers and Proceedings of the Regional Science Association, I (1955), N1-9.

13. _____ and T. Marschak. "An Activity Analysis Approach to Location Theory," Kyklos, IX (1955), 124-43.

14. Beg, Mirza Amjad. Regional Growth Points in Economic Development, with Special Reference to West Virginia. Economic Development Series, No. 8. Morgantown: West Virginia University, Bureau of Business Research, 1965.

15. Beika, Minoru. "Problems of Industrial Location Relating to Regional Development in Japan," Kobe Economic and Business Review, IX (1962), 61-68.

16. Berkman, Herman G. An Introductory Bibliography in Planning Theory. Eugene, Oregon: Council of Planning Librarians, 1965.

17. Berman, Barbara R. "Analysis of Urban Problems--Discussion," American Economic Review, LI, 2 (May, 1961), 299-300.

18. Berman, Edward B. "A Spatial and Dynamic Growth Model, Regional Science Association Papers and Proceedings, V (1959), 143-50.

19. Berry, Brian J. L. "City Size Distributions and Economic Development," Economic Development and Cultural Change, IX (July, 1961), 573-88.

20. _____, and W. L. Garrison. "Alternate Explanations of Urban Rank-Size Relationships," Annals of the Association of American Geographers, XLVIII (March, 1958).

21. _____, and Allen Pred. Central Place Studies: A Bibliography of Theory and Applications. Philadelphia: Regional Science Research Institute, 1961.

22. Blowers, Charles W. "Measuring Growth Patterns in Employment by County: A Critique," Tennessee Survey, II, 10 (June, 1967), 1-6, 14.

23. Bogue, Donald J., and Beverly Duncan. A Composite Method for Estimating Postcensal Population of Small Areas by Age, Sex, and Color. Vital Statistics, Special Reports, Selected Studies, XLVII, 6. Washington, D.C.: U.S. Public Health Service, National Office of Vital Statistics, 1959. Reprinted, 1963.

24. _____, and Dorothy L. Harris. Comparative Population and Urban Research Via Multiple Regression and Covariance Analysis. Studies in Population Distribution, No. 8. Scripps Foundation for Research in Population Problems, Miami University, Oxford, Ohio, and Population Research and Training Center, University of Chicago, 1954.

25. Borts, George H. "The Equalization of Returns and Regional Economic Growth," American Economic Review, L, 3 (June, 1960), 319-47.

26. _____, and Jerome L. Stein. Economic Growth in a Free Market. New York: Columbia University Press, 1964.

27. Boudeville, J. R. "A Survey of Recent Techniques for Regional Economic Analysis." Regional Economic Planning. Edited by Walter Isard and John H. Cumberland. Paris: Organization for European Economic Cooperation, 1961. Pp. 377-98.

28. Boventer, Edwin von. "Spatial Organization Theory as a Basis for Regional Planning," Journal of the American Institute of Planners, XXX, 2 (May, 1964), 90-100.

29. Bramhall, David F. "Projecting Regional Accounts and Industrial Locations: Reflections on Policy Applications," Regional Science Association Papers and Proceedings, VII (1961), 89-118.

30. _____, and M. Gordon Wolman. "A Note on the Small Watershed as a Planning Unit," Journal of Farm Economics, XLIII (May, 1961), 314-15.

31. Broude, Henry W. "The Significance of Regional Studies for the Elaboration of National Economic History," Journal of Economic History, XX (December, 1960), 588-96.

32. Bruno, M. P. J. Interdependence, Resource Use and Structural Change in Israel. Jerusalem: Bank of Israel Research Department, 1962.

33. Buck, T. W. "Shift and Share Analysis-- A Guide to Regional Policy?" Regional Studies, IV, 4 (December, 1970), 445-50.

34. Carrothers, Gerald A. P. "An Historical Review of the Gravity and Potential Concepts of Human Interaction," Journal of the American Institute of Planners, XXII (Spring, 1956), 94-102.

35. _____. "Population Projections by Means of Income Potential Models," Regional Science Association Papers and Proceedings, IV (1958), 121-52.

36. Chapin, F. Stuart, Jr. Urban Land Use Planning. Urbana: University of Illinois Press, 1965.

37. Chenery, Hollis B., and Paul G. Clark. Interindustry Economics. New York: Wiley and Sons, 1959.

38. Chetwynd, George. "The North East: A
Case Study in Regional Development," Lloyd's Bank
Review, LXX (October, 1963), 21-31.

39. Chinitz, Benjamin, and Raymond Vernon.
"Changing Forces in Industrial Location," Harvard
Business Review, XXXVIII, 1 (January-February,
1960), 126-36.

40. Chisholm, Michael. "Tendencies in Agricultural Specialization and Regional Concentration
of Industry," Regional Science Association Papers
and Proceedings, X (1963), 157-62.

41. Christaller, Walter. Central Places in
Southern Germany. Translated by Carlisle W. Baskin,
from Die Zentralen Orte in Suddeutschland. Englewood Cliffs, N.J.: Prentice-Hall, 1966.

42. Committee for Economic Development. Community Economic Development: Five Case Studies.
Supplementary paper, No. 18. New York: Committee
for Economic Development, 1964; New York: Frederick
A. Praeger, 1966.

43. Condliffe, John Bell. "Location in a
Planned Economy," Indian Economic Review, V (February, 1960), 58-66.

44. Conference on Regional Accounts. Werner
Hochwald, ed. Design of Regional Accounts. Papers
presented at the Conference, sponsored by the Committee on Regional Accounts. Baltimore: Johns
Hopkins Press for Resources for the Future, 1961.

45. _____, 1962. Werner Z. Hirsch, ed. Elements of Regional Accounts. Papers presented at
the Conference, sponsored by the Committee on Regional Accounts. Baltimore: Johns Hopkins Press
for Resources for the Future, 1964.

46. Cumberland, John H. "A Regional Interindustry Model for Analysis of Development Objectives," Regional Science Association Papers, XVII
(1966).

47. Czamanski, Stanislaw. Regional Income and
Product Accounts of North-Eastern Nova Scotia.
Halifax, Nova Scotia: Dalhousie University, Insti-
tute of Public Affairs, 1968.

48. _____, and Emil E. Malizia. "Applicabil-
ity and Limitations in the Use of National Input-
Output Tables for Regional Studies," The Regional
Science Association Papers, XXIII (1969), 65-77.

49. Devine, E. J. A Framework for the Analysis of Depressed Areas. Los Angeles: University of
California, Institute of Government and Public Affairs, 1964.

50. Dickinson, Robert E. City and Region:
A Geographical Interpretation. New York: Humani-
ties Press, 1964.

51. Dorfman, Robert, ed. Measuring Benefits
of Government Investment. Studies of Government
Finance. Washington, D.C.: Brookings Institute,
1965.

52. Doxiadis, Constantinos A. "Ekistics and
Regional Science," Regional Science Association
Papers and Proceedings, X (1963), 9-46.

53. Due, John F. "Studies of State-Local Tax
Influences on Location of Industry," National Tax
Journal, XIV (June, 1961), 163-73.

54. Duncan, Otis Dudley, et al. Statistical
Geography: Problems in Analyzing Area Data.
Glencoe: Free Press, 1961.

55. _____. Metropolis and Region. Baltimore:
The Johns Hopkins Press for Resources for the Future,
1960.

56. Dunn, Edgar S., Jr. "A Statistical and
Analytical Technique for Regional Analysis," Re-
gional Science Association Papers and Proceedings,
VI (1960), 97-112.

57. Dziewonski, Kazimierz. "Theoretical Problems in the Development of Economic Regions, with Special Emphasis on Poland," Regional Science Association Papers and Proceedings, Pt. 1, Vol. VIII (1962), pp. 43-54; Pt. 2, Vol. X (1963), pp. 51-60.

58. Eckaus, Richard S. "The North-South Differential in Italian Economic Development," Journal of Economic History, XXI (September, 1961), 285-317.

59. Eckstein, Otto. Water Resource Development: The Economics of Project Evaluation. Harvard Economic Studies, Vol. CIV. Cambridge: Harvard University Press, 1961.

60. Ely, Richard Theodore, and George S. Wehrwein. Land Economics. Madison: University of Wisconsin Press, 1964.

61. Fischer, Gordon Roy. "Further Calculations on Regional Differences in Profitability and Growth," Scottish Journal of Political Economy, IX (June, 1962), 147-58.

62. Fischer, Joseph L. "Concepts in Regional Economic Development Programs," Regional Science Association Papers and Proceedings, I (1955), W1-20.

63. Fox, Karl A. "The Study of Interactions Between Agriculture and the Nonfarm Economy: Local, Regional and National," Journal of Farm Economics, XLIV (February, 1962), 1-34.

64. Friedmann, John, ed. "Regional Development and Planning," special issue, Journal of the American Institute of Planners, XXX, 2 (May, 1964).

65. _____. Regional Development Policy: A Case Study of Venezuela. Cambridge: Massachusetts Institute of Technology Press, 1966.

66. _____, with discussion by J. W. Millman. "Regional Planning in Post-Industrial Society: Some Policy Considerations," Journal of Farm Economics, XLV (December, 1963), 1073-82.

67. _____, and W. Alonso, eds. Regional Development and Planning. Cambridge: Massachusetts Institute of Technology Press, 1964.

68. Fuchs, Victor Robert. "Statistical Explanations of the Relative Shift of Manufacturing Among Regions of the United States," Regional Science Association Papers and Proceedings, VIII (1962), 105-26.

69. Gallaway, Lowell Eugene. "An Economic Analysis of Public Policy for the Depressed Areas," Industrial and Labor Relations Review, XV (July, 1962), 500-09.

70. _____. "Proposals for Federal Aid to Depressed Industrial Areas: A Critique," Industrial and Labor Relations Review, XIV (April, 1961), 363-78.

71. Glasgow, Robert B., and Emanuel L. Baum, with discussion by W. W. McPherson. "Considerations for Planning of Economic Development of Rural Areas," Journal of Farm Economics, XLV (December, 1963), 1083-91.

72. Goldman, Morris R., Martin L. Marimont, and Beatrice N. Vaccara. "The Interindustry Structure of the United States," Survey of Current Business, XLIV, 11 (November, 1964), 10-30.

73. Greenhut, Melvin L. "An Explanation of Industrial Development in Underdeveloped Areas of the United States," Land Economics, XXXVI (November, 1960), 371-79.

74. _____. Plant Location in Theory and in Practice: The Economics of Space. Chapel Hill: University of North Carolina Press, 1956.

75. _____. "Size of Markets Versus Transportation Costs in Industrial Location Surveys and Theory," Journal of Industrial Economics, VIII (March, 1960), 172-84.

76. Haggett, Peter. Locational Analysis in Human Geography. New York: St. Martin's Press, 1966.

77. Hagood, M. J. "Statistical Methods for Delineation of Regions Applied to Data on Agriculture and Population," Social Forces, XXI (March, 1943), 287-97.

78. Hammer, Thomas. The Estimation of Economic Base Multipliers. RSRI Discussion Paper Series, No. 22. Philadelphia: Regional Science Research Institute, 1968.

79. Hansen, William Lee, and Charles M. Tiebout. "An Intersectoral Flows Analysis of the California Economy," Review of Economics and Statistics, XLV, 4 (November, 1963), 409-18.

80. Harris, Britton. "Analysis of Urban Problems--Discussion," American Economic Review, LI, 2 (May, 1961), 301-2.

81. _____. "Plan or Projection: An Examination of the Use of Models in Planning," Journal of the American Institute of Planners, XXVI (November, 1960), 265-72.

82. Hart, P. E., and Alasdair I. MacBean. "Regional Differences in Productivity, Profitability, and Growth: A Pilot Study," Scottish Journal of Political Economy, VIII (February, 1961), 1-11.

83. Henderson, James. "An Economic Analysis of the Upper-Midwest Region." Four Papers on Methodology. Upper Midwest Economic Study Technical Papers, No. 1. June, 1961. Pp. 1-22.

84. _____, and Anne O. Krueger. National Growth and Economic Change in the Upper Midwest. Minneapolis: University of Minnesota Press, 1965.

85. Hermann, Frank V. _Population Forecasting Methods: A Report on Forecasting and Estimating Methods_. Revised edition. Washington, D.C.: U.S. Bureau of Public Roads, 1964.

86. Hermansen, Tormod. _Interregional Allocation of Investments for Social and Economic Development_. Geneva: U.N. Research Institute for Social Development, 1970.

87. Hill, Forest G. "Regional Aspects of Economic Development," _Land Economics_, XXXVIII (May, 1962), 85-98.

88. Hirsch, Werner Z. "Design and Use of Regional Accounts," _American Economic Review_, LII (May, 1962), 365-73.

89. _____. "Regional Fiscal Impact of Local Industrial Development," _Regional Science Association Papers and Proceedings_, VII (1961), 119-30.

90. _____, and Sidney Sonenblum. _Selecting Regional Information for Government Planning and Decision-Making_. New York: Praeger Publishers, 1970.

91. Hochwald, Werner. "Conceptual Issues of Regional Income Estimation." _Regional Income_. Studies in Income and Wealth, XXI, National Bureau of Economic Research. Princeton: Princeton University Press, 1957. Pp. 9-26.

92. _____, et al. _Local Impact of Foreign Trade: A Study in Methods of Local Economic Accounting_. Washington, D.C.: National Planning Association, 1960.

93. Hoover, Edgar M. _The Location of Economic Activity_. New York: McGraw-Hill, 1948.

94. Houston, David B. "The Shift and Share Analysis of Regional Growth: A Critique," _The Southern Economic Journal_, XXXIII, 4 (April, 1967), 577-81.

95. Hoyt, Homer H. "A Method for Measuring the Value of Imports Into an Urban Community," Land Economics, XXXVII (May, 1961), 150-61.

96. _____. "Economic Background of Cities," Journal of Land and Public Utilities Economics, XVII (May, 1964), 188-95.

97. Hughes, Rufus Britton, Jr. "Interregional Income Differences: Self-Perpetuation," Southern Economic Journal, XXVIII (July, 1961), 41-45.

98. Hurter, Arthur P., and Leon M. Moses. "Transportation Investment and Regional Development," Journal of the American Institute of Planners, XXX, 2 (May, 1964), 132-39.

99. Isard, Walter. "Interregional and Regional Input-Output Analysis: A Model of a Space-Economy," Review of Economics and Statistics, XXXIII (November, 1951), 318-28.

100. _____. Location and Space Economy. New York: Massachusetts Institute of Technology and Wiley, 1956.

101. _____. Methods of Regional Analysis: An Introduction to Regional Science. New York: Massachusetts Institute of Technology and Wiley, 1960.

102. _____. "Regional Commodity Balances and Interregional Commodity Flows," American Economic Review, XLIII (May, 1953), 167-80.

103. _____. "Some Empirical Results and Problems of Regional Input-Output Analysis." Studies in the Structure of the American Economy. Wasily W. Leontief, ed. New York: Oxford University Press, 1953.

104. _____, and John H. Cumberland, eds. Regional Economic Planning. Paris: Organization for European Economic Cooperation, 1961.

105. _____, and David Ostroff. "The Existence of a Competitive Interregional Equilibrium," Regional Science Association Papers and Proceedings, IV (1958), 49-76.

106. _____, Eugene W. Schooler, and Thomas Vietorisz. Industrial Complex Analysis and Regional Development: A Case Study of Refinery-Petrochemical-Synthetic-Fiber Complexes and Puerto Rico. Cambridge: Massachusetts Institute of Technology, 1959.

107. Israel Delegation to the OECD Seminar on Regional Development. Regional Development in Israel. Jerusalem: The Delegation, 1964.

108. Jaffe, A. J. Handbook of Statistical Methods of Demographers: Selected Problems in the Analysis of Census Data. Washington, D.C.: U.S. Bureau of the Census, 1960.

109. Jaszi, George, et al. Readings in Concepts and Methods of National Income Statistics. Washington, D.C.: U.S. Department of Commerce, Office of Business Economics, 1970.

110. Jones, Barclay G., and William W. Goldsmith. Studies in Regional Development: A Factor Analysis Approach to Sub-Regional Definition in Chenango, Delaware, and Otsego Counties (New York). Ithaca, N.Y.: Cornell University, Center for Housing and Environmental Studies, Division of Urban Studies, 1965.

111. _____, et al. Regional Analysis for Economic Development: A Demonstration Study of Schoharie County, New York. Ithaca, N.Y.: Cornell University, Center for Housing and Environmental Studies, Division of Urban Studies, 1964.

112. Kawalec, W. "Regional Statistics for Planning Requirements." Paper presented at the Conference of European Statisticians, Prague, 1967.

113. Klaassen, Leon H., Wim C. Kroft, and
Reinier Voskuil. "Regional Income Differences in
Holland," Regional Science Association Papers and
Proceedings, X (1963), 77-81.

114. Kruczala, Jerzy. "The Attempt to Formu-
late the Theoretical Base of Regional Science,"
Regional Science Association Papers and Proceedings,
X (1963), 47-49.

115. Krutilla, John V., and Otto Eckstein.
Multiple Purpose River Development: Studies in Ap-
plied Economic Analysis. Baltimore: Johns Hopkins
Press for Resources for the Future, 1958.

116. Lefeber, Louis. Allocation in Space:
Production, Transport, and Industrial Location.
Amsterdam: North-Holland Publishing Company, 1958.

117. _____. "General Equilibrium Analysis of
Production Transportation, and the Choice of Industrial Location," Regional Science Association Papers
and Proceedings, IV (1958), 77-89.

118. Leontief, Wassily W. "Some Basic Problems of Empirical Input-Output Analysis," Input-
Output Analysis: An Appraisal. Studies in Income
and Wealth, Vol. XVIII. National Bureau of Economic
Research. Princeton: Princeton University Press,
1955.

119. _____. "The Structure of Development,"
Scientific American, CCIX, 23 (September, 1963)
148-66.

120. Leven, Charles L. "A Theory of Social
Accounting," Regional Science Association Papers
and Proceedings, IV (1958), 221-37.

121. _____. "Establishing Goals for Regional
Economic Development," Journal of the American Institute of Planners, XXX, 2 (May, 1964), 100-10.

122. _____. "Regional and Interregional Accounts in Perspective," <u>Regional Science Association Papers and Proceedings</u>, XIII (1964), 127-44.

123. _____. <u>Theory and Method of Income and Product Accounts for Metropolitan Areas, Including the Elgin-Dundee Area as a Case Study</u>. Ames, Iowa: Iowa State College, 1958.

124. _____, et al. <u>An Analytical Framework for Regional Development Policy</u>. Cambridge: Massachusetts Institute of Technology Press, 1970.

125. Lösch, August, <u>The Economics of Location</u>. Translated from the second revised edition by W. H. Woglom. New Haven: Yale University Press, 1954.

126. Maki, Wilbur R., and Yien I. Tu. "Regional Growth Models for Rural Areas Development," <u>Regional Science Association Papers and Proceedings</u>, IX (1962), 235-44.

127. Melamid, Alexander. "Regional Analysis of Resources and Growth," <u>Social Research</u>, XXIX (January, 1963), 495-98.

128. Miernyk, William H. <u>The Elements of Input-Output Analysis</u>. New York: Random House, 1965.

129. _____, et al. <u>Impact of the Space Program on a Local Economy</u>. Morgantown: West Virginia University Library, 1967.

130. _____. <u>Simulating Regional Economic Development</u>. Lexington, Mass.: Heath Lexington Books, 1970.

131. Moses, Leon N. "An Input-Output Linear Programming Approach to Interregional Analysis." <u>Report, 1956-57</u>. Cambridge: Harvard Economic Research Project, 1957.

132. _____. "The Stability of Interregional Trading Patterns and Input-Output Analysis," _American Economic Review_, XLV (December, 1955), 803-32.

133. National Bureau of Economic Research. _Regional Income_. Studies in Income and Wealth, Vol. XXI. Princeton: Princeton University Press, 1957.

134. Needleman, L., ed. _Regional Analysis_. Harmondsworth, England: Penguin Books, 1968.

135. Nicholls, William H. "Industrialization, Factor Markets, and Agricultural Development," _Journal of Political Economy_, LXIX (August, 1961), 319-40.

136. Nichols, Vida. _Growth Poles: An Investigation of Their Potential as a Tool for Regional Economic Development_. RSRI Discussion Paper Series, No. 30. Philadelphia: Regional Science Research Institute, 1969.

137. Nourse, Hugh. _Regional Economics_. New York: McGraw-Hill, 1968.

138. O'Donnell, John L., _et al_. _Economic and Population Case Study of the Lansing Tri-County Area: An Inter-Industry Relations Analysis_. East Lansing: Michigan State University, Bureau of Business and Economic Research, 1960.

139. Okun, Bernard, and Richard W. Richardson. "Regional Income Inequality and Internal Population Migrations," _Economic Development and Cultural Change_, IX (January, 1961), 128-43.

140. Perloff, Harvey S. "Problems of Assessing Regional Economic Progress." _Regional Income_. Studies in Income and Wealth, Vol. XXI. Princeton: National Bureau of Economic Research, Princeton University Press, 1957. Pp. 35-62.

141. _____, and Vera W. Dodds. _How a Region Grows: Area Development in the U.S. Economy_. New York: Committee for Economic Development, 1963.

142. _____, et al. Regions, Resources, and
Economic Growth. Baltimore: Johns Hopkins Press
for Resources for the Future, 1960.

143. Pfouts, Ralph W., ed. The Techniques of
Urban Economic Analysis. Trenton, N.J.: Chandler-
Davis, 1960.

144. Philbrick, Allen K. "Areal Functional
Organization in Regional Geography," Regional Science Association Papers and Proceedings, III (1957),
87-98.

145. Rahman, M. Anisur. "A Linear Programme
Model for Investment Allocation Between Regions or
Sectors," Pakistan Economic Journal, XII, 4 (Decem-
ber, 1962), 14-21.

146. _____. "Regional Allocation of Investment: An Aggregate Study in the Theory of Development Programming," Quarterly Journal of Economics,
LXXVII (February, 1963), 26-39.

147. Regional Economic Development Institute,
Incorporated. Technique for Area Planning. Wash-
ington, D.C.: U.S. Department of Commerce, Economic
Development Administration, 1967.

148. Reifler, Roger, and Charles M. Tiebout.
"Interregional Input-Output: An Empirical
California-Washington Model," Journal of Regional
Science, X, 2 (August, 1970), 135-52.

149. Resources for the Future. Design for a
Worldwide Study of Regional Development. A report
to the United Nations on a proposed research-
training program. Baltimore: Johns Hopkins Press,
1966.

150. Robock, Stefan H. Brazil's Developing
Northeast: A Study of Regional Planning and Foreign Aid. Washington, D.C.: Brookings Institution,
1963.

151. Ruttan, Vernon Wesley, and Luther Tompkins Wallace. "The Effectiveness of Location Incentives on Local Economic Development," Journal of Farm Economics, XLIV (November, 1962), 968-78.

152. Schaffer, William A., and Kong Chu. "Nonsurvey Techniques for Constructing Regional Interindustry Models," The Regional Science Association Papers, XXIII (1969), 83-101.

153. Schmitt, Robert C. Bibliography of Methodological Studies in Small-Area Population Estimation and Projection Issued Since 1945. Eugene, Oregon: Council of Planning Librarians, 1962.

154. Siebert, Horst. Regional Economic Growth: Theory and Policy. Scranton, Pa.: International Textbook Company, 1969.

155. Sonenblum, Sidney, and Louis H. Stern. "The Use of Economic Projections in Planning," Journal of the American Institute of Planners, XXX, 2 (May, 1964), 110-23.

156. Spiegelman, Robert G. Review of Techniques of Regional Analysis with Particular Emphasis on Applicability of Those Techniques to Regional Problems. SRI Project No. 532-531-4. Menlo Park: Stanford Research Institute, 1962.

157. Spiegelmann, Robert H., et al. Application of Activity Analysis to Regional Development Planning: A Case Study of Economic Planning in Rural South Central Kentucky. Technical Bulletin No. 1339. Washington, D.C.: U.S. Department of Agriculture, Economic Research Service, 1965.

158. Stilwell, F. B. J. "Further Thoughts on the Shift and Share Approach," Regional Studies, IV, 4 (December, 1970), 451-58.

159. _____, and B. D. Boatwright. "A Method of Estimating Interregional Trade Flows," Regional and Urban Economics, I, 1 (May, 1971), 77-87.

160. Stohr, Walter. "Planning for Depressed Areas: A Methodological Approach," Journal of the American Institute of Planners, XXX, 2 (May, 1964), 123-31.

161. Stone, Richard. "Social Accounts of the Regional Level: A Survey." Regional Economic Planning. W. Isard and J. H. Cumberland, eds. Paris: Organization for European Economic Cooperation, 1961. Pp. 263-93.

162. Teitz, Michael B. "Regional Theory and Regional Models," Regional Science Association Papers and Proceedings, IX (1962), 35-50.

163. Thomas, Morgan D. "Economic Activity in Small Areas," Land Economics, XXXVI (May, 1960), 164-71.

164. _____. "Regional Economic Growth and Industrial Development," Regional Science Association Papers and Proceedings, X (1963), 61-75.

165. _____. "The Economic Base and a Region's Economy," Journal of the American Institute of Planners, XXIII, 2 (1957).

166. Thompson, Lorin A. "Appraisal of Alternative Methods of Estimating Local Area Income." Regional Income. Studies in Income and Wealth, Vol. XXI. Princeton: Princeton University Press, 1957.

167. Thompson, Wilbur R. A Preface to Urban Economics. Baltimore: Johns Hopkins Press for Resources for the Future, 1965.

168. Tiebout, Charles M. The Community Economic Base Study. Supplementary Paper No. 16. New York: Committee for Economic Development, 1962.

169. _____. "Exports and Regional Economic Growth," Journal of Political Economy, LXIV (April, 1956).

170. _____. "Regional and Interregional Input-Output Models: An Appraisal," The Southern Economic Journal, XXIV, 2 (October, 1957), 140-47.

171. Tolley, George S., and Fletcher E. Riggs, eds. Economics of Watershed Plannings. Ames: Iowa State University Press, 1961.

172. Ullman, Edward, and Michael Dacey. "The Minimum Requirements Approach to the Urban Economic Base," Regional Science Association Papers and Proceedings, VI (1960), 175-94.

173. U.N. Research Institute for Social Development. Case Studies in Information Systems for Regional Development. Vol. I, Tormod Hermansen, Sweden; Vol. II, Sergio Boisier, Chile; India and Poland forthcoming. Geneva: U.N. Research Institute for Social Development, 1970.

174. U.S. Department of Commerce, Office of Business Economics. Growth Patterns in Employment by County, 1940-50 and 1950-60. Washington, D.C.: U.S. Government Printing Office, 1966.

175. _____. National Income. (A supplement to Survey of Current Business.) Washington, D.C.: U.S. Department of Commerce, 1954.

176. _____. U.S. Income and Output. (A supplement to Survey of Current Business.) Washington, D.C.: U.S. Department of Commerce, 1958.

177. U.S. Department of Health, Education, and Welfare. Toward a Social Report. Washington, D.C.: U.S. Government Printing Office, 1969.

178. University of California at Los Angeles, School of Business Administration, Division of Research. Industrial Location Bibliography. Los Angeles: University of Los Angeles, 1959.

179. University of Colorado, Bureau of Economic Research. The Impact of Space and Space-Related Activities on a Local Economy. Part 1, The Input-Output Analysis; Part 2, The Income-Product Accounts. Boulder: University of Colorado, Institute of Behavioral Research, Bureau of Economic Research, 1965.

180. Upper Midwest Economic Study. James M. Henderson, Anne O. Krueger, et al. National Growth and Economic Change in the Upper Midwest. Final report of the study. Minneapolis: University of Minnesota Press, 1965.

181. Vernon, Raymond. The Changing Economic Function of the Central City. Supplementary Paper, No. 6. New York: Committee for Economic Development, 1959.

182. Vining, Rutledge. "A Description of Certain Spatial Aspects of an Economic System," Economic Development and Cultural Change, III (January, 1955).

183. _____. "Delimitation of Economic Areas: Statistical Conceptions in the Study of the Spatial Structure of an Economic System," Journal of the American Statistical Association, XLVII (January, 1953), 44-64.

184. _____. "Location of Industry and Regional Patterns of Business-Behavior," Econometrica, XIV (July, 1946).

185. _____. "The Region as an Economic Entity and Certain Variations to be Observed in the Study of Systems of Regions," American Economic Review, XXXIX (May, 1949), 89-104.

186. Weiss, Steven J., and Edwin C. Gooding. "Estimation of Differential Employment Multipliers in a Small Regional Economy," Land Economics, XLIV, 2 (May, 1968), 235-44.

187. Western Committee on Regional Economic Analysis. _Interregional Linkages_. Berkeley: The Committee, 1954.

188. Williamson, Jeffrey G. "Regional Inequality and the Process of National Development: A Description of the Patterns," _Economic Development and Cultural Change_, Vol. XIII, No. 4, Pt. 2 (July, 1965).

189. Wilson, Thomas, ed. _Papers on Regional Development: Supplement to the Journal of Industrial Economics_. Oxford: Basil Blackwell, 1965.

190. _____. Policies for Regional Development_. University of Glasgow, Social and Economic Studies, Occasional Papers, No. 3. Edinburgh: Oliver and Boyd, 1964.

191. Wolff, P., and P. E. Venekamp. "On a System of Regional Social Accounts for the City of Amsterdam," _International Statistical Institute Bulletin_, Vol. XXXV, Pt. 4 (1957).

192. Wrobel, Andrzej. "Regional Analysis and the Geographic Concept of Region," _Regional Science Association Papers and Proceedings_, VIII (1962), 37-41.

Periodicals

1. _Economic Development and Cultural Change_. Chicago: University of Chicago Press (University of Chicago, Research Center for Economic Development and Cultural Change).

2. _Ekistics_. Reviews on problems and science of human settlements.) Athens: Doxiadis Associates.

3. _Journal of Regional Science_. Philadelphia: Regional Science Research Institute.

4. <u>Journal of the American Institute of Planners</u>. Washington, D.C.: American Institute of Planners.

5. <u>Land Economics</u>. Madison, Wisconsin: University of Wisconsin Press.

6. <u>Quarterly Digest of Urban and Regional Research</u>. Urbana: University of Illinois Press.

7. <u>Regional and Urban Economics (Operational Methods)</u>. Amsterdam: North-Holland Publishing Company.

8. <u>Regional Studies</u>. Oxford, England: Regional Studies Association and Pergamon Press, Ltd.

9. <u>The Regional Science Association Papers</u>. Philadelphia: The Regional Science Association and University of Pennsylvania.

10. <u>Review of Regional Studies</u>. Blacksburg, Virginia: Virginia Polytechnic Institute and State University.

AVROM BENDAVID is Team Regional Economist for the UN/IPD Team for the Development of the Northern Region, Thailand. Prior to this he was Staff Regional Economist of the Settlement Study Centre, Rehovot, Israel, and lectured on regional economics and methods of regional analysis within the framework of the International Course in Comprehensive Regional Development Planning conducted there. He was formerly a consultant in regional development for a private firm in the United States and has taught economics at the University of Maryland.

Mr. Bendavid has had considerable experience in the collection, processing, and analysis of regional data; the organization, staffing, training, and activation of local development staffs; enlistment of public support for development programs; preparation of over-all economic development programs; action planning; plan implementation; the drafting of regional cooperation legislation; program evaluation; and other aspects of regional research and planning for development. He has worked with regional research and development teams from a number of different countries and has been involved in the training of regional development personnel from developing countries in Africa, Asia, Latin America, and the Middle East, as well as from lagging regions in the United States.

Mr. Bendavid did his post-graduate work in regional and development economics at the University of Maryland.